CHESI

Other titles by the author

Chaldon Herring: Writers in a Dorset Landscape

A Dorset Utopia: The Little Commonwealth and Homer Lane

Under Black Ven: Mary Anning's Story

Weymouth & Mr. Punch

The Way to Do It: Frank Edmonds Punch & Judy Man

Boo to a Goose

Tom's Tale

The Apple-Tree Man

The Hurley Giants

CHESIL BEACH
a peopled solitude

Judith Stinton

HARLEQUIN PRESS

First published in 2021 by Harlequin Press
www.harlequinpress.net

Designed and typeset in Minion Pro by Philip Lord

Printed and bound by
Short Run Press, Exeter

ISBN 978-0-9559224-2-8

Reprinted November 2021

Acknowledgements

I would like to thank, first and foremost, the staff of Dorset History Centre; Shirley Mitchell and Portland Heritage Trust Study Centre; Bridport Museum and Local History Centre; and Weymouth Reference Library.

Thanks go to Judith Bond, who has walked the terrain with me, enduring mud and several wild goose chases – and to Mick Orr for his photographs, and his patience in exploring the more unlovely parts of Weymouth. I'm grateful to Frances Nicholson for her help with the bibliography and proofs, and to Kate Hebditch for her advice. And thanks to David Brown for his cover photograph. I would especially like to thank Philip Lord for designing the book.

I also wish to acknowledge the help of Hadlee Bennett, Janey and Francis Carline, Val Dicker, Peter Gill, Jo Hearton, Brother Hugh SSF, Debbie Hughes, Peter Kemp, Charles Lock, Anna Lord, Stephen Mottram, Tom Neilson, Peter Tolhurst and John Willows.

Judith Stinton, 2021

ILLUSTRATIONS

David Brown, front cover, 224; Mick Orr, frontispiece, 27, 174, 205, back cover; Dorset History Centre 19, 32, 84; Dorset County Museum 38, 103, 143, 160, 217, 223, 263; Portland Heritage Trust, 79, 185; Weymouth Library, 201

To Judith Bond,
who walked this book

*Chesil Beach from Portland Heights (*Mick Orr*).*

CONTENTS

FOREWORD

FROM THE HEIGHTS OF PORTLAND, looking down into Lyme Bay, the Chesil Beach slowly unwinds. On a calm day, the watcher has a gull's eye view of this strong and stony barrier of pebbles, snaking into the horizon. On the landward side the Beach is flanked by the Fleet lagoon; on the far side it slides into the sea's frivolous and lacy fringe of foam.

Lagoon and Beach are a highly unusual combination. When considered together with Abbotsbury Swannery, they are unique. Chesil Beach also forms part of a World Heritage Site, known as the Jurassic Coast, an entirely natural phenomenon stretching from Studland Bay in Dorset to Exmouth in Devon – a westward journey back through 185 million years of time.

Chesil Beach itself, although it looks so ancient, is not old in geological time. Nor is it as static as it might seem. Shape-shifting, self-renewing, Chesil Beach is continually on the move, and the movement is inwards.

Beyond the industrial strip along Portland's causeway and the caravans and army camp at Wyke Regis, the coast looks empty and unpopulated; the villages have retreated inland. Yet there are people here, and have been for centuries, leading their private lives behind the shingle bank.

(The old name for the Beach was Chesil Bank, which was a useful way of distinguishing shingle from shoreline.) Without the Bank's protection there would be no Weymouth.

Clandestine activities have abounded along this coast: while poaching, smuggling and wrecking might be predictable occupations, there have also been undercover meetings of spies and hush-hush weapon testing. D-Day soldiers left from here for France. The Armada sailed menacingly through its waters.

The solitude and silence have attracted idealistic communities. John Middleton Murry experimented with a writers' colony at Abbotsbury, while Adela Curtis founded a longer-lasting sisterhood of White Ladies outside Burton Bradstock.

Some activities had further-reaching consequences, both for England and for countries as distant as Spain and Russia – this history is not just local. And while there are many excellent books on the geology, flora, fauna and ornithology of the Chesil and the Fleet, the lives of those other specimens – the inhabitants – have received scant attention.

What most people did most of the time, of course, was work, and most of their work involved sea-fishing. The sea, their constant companion, could provide rich pickings. But water was their enemy too – a terrifying and destructive force. And of all the happenings along this extraordinary length of coast the most disastrous was a devastating storm in the early nineteenth century: the only occasion on which the sea broke through the shingle of Chesil Beach

The Moons and the Fleet

Blow wind, rise storm,
Ship ashore before morn.

On the night of Monday November 22nd 1824, a hurricane blew up along the south-west coast, badly affecting Dorset and battering Lyme Bay. In Lyme Regis harbour 'the sea ran through [the Cobb] in a manner truly appalling, and soon swept every vessel out'. The *Colyton Regis* came to grief there, and the *Colville* foundered in West Bay. In Wyke Regis the Ferry House was destroyed, killing two people, while in Weymouth Bay the huge stone blocks and iron chains of the Esplanade vanished into the wild waves, and the basements of the seafront terraces were flooded. The *Amyntas* was lost off the Weymouth shore.

It was a bitter misfortune to be at sea that morning. Among other ships wrecked in Lyme Bay was the Danish West Indiaman *Carvalho*, which became grounded on the Chesil. Her entire crew was drowned, and her cargo of gin, rum and cotton was strewn along the shore. The 90 ton sloop HMS *Ebenezer* fared better. Thrown up onto the Chesil at its Portland end, she was safely relaunched on the far side of the causeway.

It was said that the waves battered Chesil Bank so remorselessly that the sea breached the bank of pebbles 'below Langton', perhaps the only time that this has ever happened. (Usually the waves go over the top of the bank, or leach through the stones.) On this occasion the Chesil offered little protection from the strength of the storm.

The best-remembered casualty of the Great Gale – the Great Outrage – was the village of East Fleet, which of all the villages along the Chesil lay closest to the shore. Other villages occupy higher ground, turning their backs on the sea. East Fleet, though, was low-lying, and when the waters of the lagoon rose by twenty feet they poured over into the sea-meadows, destroying five cottages and leaving only the chancel of the old church. The boundary stones were also washed away. It was a devastating morning from which the village never really recovered (a fire in 1935 completed the damage). The old coast road to Fleet House was abandoned for a new, more sheltered inland route.

The village became a curiosity overnight, and the visitors continued to come. More than fifty years later in 1897, a hundred worthies from the Dorset Natural History and Archaeology Field Club made an excursion to East Fleet. They were driven down to the manor house, and then taken by trow across the Fleet to Chesil Bank where, huddled on the crest of the pebbles, they listened to a talk by the geographer Vaughan Cornish on 'The Grading of the Chesil Beach Shingle'.

Afterwards, members adjourned to the old church to hear the Reverend William Miles Barnes (son of William Barnes the poet) read a paper on some of his local ecclesiastical studies. He also had information of more immediate interest to his listeners on the subject of the Great Gale.

> A few minutes ago I met in the churchyard of the old church, James Bowering, aged 87, possibly he is here now. [He was.] He is the only man living who saw the waves come up. At six o'clock on the morning of the 23rd he was standing, with other boys, by the gate near the cattle–pound when he saw, rushing up the valley the tidal wave, driven by a hurricane, and bearing on the crest a whole haystack and *débris* from the fields below. They ran for their lives to Chickerell, and when they returned they found that five houses had been swept away and the church was in ruins. Three years later the new church was commenced. In the tower of the new church is a little tablet recording the destruction of the old church and the building of the new...

In the meantime, for some years the villagers had to make do with worshipping in the neighbouring churches. A note in Wyke Regis church register records the baptism on August 6th 1826 of the son of James Gibb, revenue officer of Fleet. 'This child was baptized in this church in consequence of the church of Fleet having been destroy'd.'

The forlorn rump of the old church was patched up and left alone, to be used as a mortuary chapel, over which ivy grew in abundance. The members of the Field Club must have surely more than filled it at their action-packed 1897 meeting. (The full-day's programme was rounded off with the opportunity to see some photographs of 'zebra-horse hybrids'.) But it wasn't until after the publication a year later of John Meade Falkner's novel *Moonfleet*, that the village was brought back to a sort of life.

Born in Manningfold Bruce, Wiltshire, in 1858, Falkner spent his childhood in Dorchester and later in Weymouth, where his father, an unsuccessful cleric, was senior curate at St Mary's Church. (In 1881 he became curate-in-charge at Buckland Ripers, a mile or two inland from East Fleet.) The family lived at the Georgian rectory in Trinity Street, not much more than a pebble's throw from the sea. In his recollections of his early life, affectionate, witty and poignant, Falkner tells of Solomon Sly, 'a person of great geniality and great bulk' and of his inn, the Cutter, on Weymouth Esplanade.

> It was a 'shy' place but a light in its upper window would be very visible to boats at sea. About it hung a smuggling atmosphere which was prevalent enough in Weymouth in those days; tradition still affixed a label of 'contraband' to certain houses on the harbour, and on the 'front', and on the Backwater, and the Cutter was duly labelled... It was said that neither Customhouse nor Constable saw any reason why they would disturb so innocent and orderly a place.

Weymouth harbour was close by too, and rich with ships: sloops and schooners, ketches and cutters, of the kinds which Falkner observes in *Moonfleet* with a sea-doggish eye. Material for a smuggling novel was on his doorstep.

In writing the novel, Falkner appears to have been

influenced by Robert Louis Stevenson's *Kidnapped*, published in 1886, and an immediate success. Both books occupy that uneasy territory (now fashionable) between children's and adults' books. They are adventure stories, narrated by their boy heroes, who are both orphans.

Kidnapped begins in 1751 in the aftermath of the Jacobite Rebellion of Forty-five. Young David Balfour, heir to the house of Shaws, is tricked into boarding a brig by the machinations of his miserly uncle Ebenezer. The ship is bound for the Carolinas, and he is intended for the life of a slave. During the voyage, the brig runs into another boat, and the sole survivor of the collision climbs aboard. He is the Jacobite Alan Breck Stewart, a fighting peacock of a man, who takes David under his wing. The pair soon gain control of the chaotically captained ship, killing crew members in self-defence. There is a shipwreck, a flight through the heather and a triumphant ending. Stevenson handles this racy, picaresque tale with great aplomb, and in confident detail.

While containing many of the same elements as Stevenson's story, Falkner's novel unfolds elegantly in a series of big dramatic scenes. The book opens in the old village of Moonfleet. The narrator, fifteen-year-old John Trenchard, remarks on the village's name:

> When I was a child I thought that this place was called Moonfleet, because on a still night, whether in summer, or in winter frosts, the moon shone very brightly on the lagoon; but learned afterwards that 'twas but short for 'Mohune-fleet', from the Mohunes, a great family who were once lords of all these parts.

The year is 1757, and the month October. It was, inciden tally, a year in which the legend says that a red-haired merman was washed up on the Fleet shore after gale force winds had hit the coast.

Come the dawn, the storm was over
The wind had dropped, the sea
was calm.
Here and there
along the pebbles' sloping fortress,
figures stoop, intently combing,
among the tributes of the night.
Corals, pink as frilled flamingos,
Silver ingots
Sea-battered boots.
All are stranded
Dredged in sand.

And this other
creature of the ocean:
The forked tail and swoln
figure-head of a man.
Watch the waters seeping from him
Through the stony grated beach.
Braving the bank, he lies defeated.
For the storm he brought over our heads
has killed him:
dead he is, adorned in treasure newly-minted
of green and gold.
Yet pitye the poor merman, as we

cast his scaly carcass
back into the sea.

Judith Stinton, 'At Dawn, Chesil Beach'

Unhappily – though even more curiously – it was afterwards claimed that the creature was not a merman, but a water–logged camel, left sodden on the shore.

1757 proves to be a momentous time for John Trenchard too, as it is the year in which his life is irretrievably changed. Stepping out from his aunt's house into the village street one evening, the boy hears the sound of tap-tap-tapping. It is Ratsey Maskew, the sexton, carving a slab in Portland stone to the memory of David Block, a boy of John's age who has been killed 'by a shot fired from the *Elector* Schooner'. David was with his father Elzevir when he was shot. The elder Block is the landlord of the village inn, formerly called the Mohune Arms, but now 'in jest' renamed the Why Not?

The inn may have once existed. In a small undated leaflet which accompanied the Puffin edition of *Moonfleet,* George H Atkins (a Chickerell church warden) claims intriguingly that building operations at the southern end of the village street unearthed evidence of an eighteenth century inn. The jest however is Falkner's. For his purposes the Mohune family shield bears a 'great black Y' – 'what heralds call a *cross-pall*' – and this Y has given the inn its name, while also providing a refrain for the book.

The design of the shield is an invention of Falkner's. In his monumental history of Dorset (1861–70) John Hutchins, chronicler of the great families of the county, their lineage,

Early postcard. Old cottage, Fleet. "The Why Not of Moonfleet".

their lands and their coats of arms, describes the Mohune's shield as 'Arms: Gules, a man's arm inhabited in a maunch ermine, the hand proper holding a fleur de lys or, within a border argent'. That is, the shield shows an arm clad in a dangling sleeve, with the hand holding a flower, on a red background. The sleeve is shaped as an 'M', indicating that the family came from La Manche in France, but also of course standing for 'Mohune'. *Manche* in French means *sleeve*, so by replacing the M by a Y, Falkner has quietly exchanged one pun for another. 'Cantling arms' as such puns are known, are a popular feature of heraldry. *Cant* is a word for a secret language (most commonly used to describe the tongue once used by thieves and beggars.)

A scholarly and learned man, Falkner was fascinated by the arcane vocabulary of heraldry, which he also employed in his two other novels (a fourth novel was reportedly left on a train). In the earlier *Lost Stradivarius*, published three years before *Moonfleet*, the ill-fated violin's case is stamped with a 'florid foreign blazon' which bodes no good for its owners. Even the title of his most elaborate fiction, *The Nebuly Coat* (1903) is armorial, and the coat, a 'barry nebuly of six, argent and vert' (that is, 'silver-white crossed by waving sea-green bars') is a sinister feature of the book.

The Mohunes were lords of the manor of Fleet from 1566 – when the estate was conveyed to 'Robert Moone or Mohun' – until 1774, when it was passed by marriage to the Gould family. George Gould was rector at the time of the Great Gale. He gave shelter to villagers who had lost their homes in the tidal wave, and was responsible for the building of the new church. George Gould and his cousins also built the small south lodge and the great new gateway when, as a result of the flooding, the old track up the hill became the new approach to Fleet House. Two grand stone piers were erected, each surmounted by a lion. The limestone came from the same Upwey quarry and was of the same fine quality as that used for his church. The stateliness of this entrance was somewhat diminished during the Second World War when one of the pillars, along with one of the wrought-iron gates which closed the road, was removed by American troops to enable them to manoeuvre their vehicles through the gateway. A lion was left forlornly sitting on the wall, where it can still be seen. (A later north lodge, on the parish boundary between Fleet and Chickerell, waves a banner for the Goulds.)

The Mohune family were once scattered around Dorset. Another, more major branch held Ham Mohun ('vulgarly called Hammoon' according to Hutchins's *History of Dorset*) in the north of the county. There are even rumours of a vanished castle, somewhere near the Devon border. The Mohunes still owned the Fleet estate at the time of the story, but are said by Falkner to be in decline. Their fortunes had fallen and 'with them fell the fortunes of Moonfleet. The ruins of their mansion showed grey on the hillside above the village; their almshouses stood half-way down the street, with the quadrangle deserted and overgrown; the Mohune image and inscription was on everything from the church to the inn, and everything that bore it was stamped also with the superscription of decay'.

One long-dead member of the family, buried in the chancel vault, is said to walk 'on the first nights of winter'. He is Colonel John Mohune, known as 'Blackbeard', a man tormented by his own wickedness: 'he must have been bad indeed, for Mohunes have died before and since his day wicked enough to bear anyone company in their vault or elsewhere'. In the novel he is reported as having 'deserted the allegiance of his house and supported the cause of the rebels' during 'the dreadful wars against King Charles the First'. In fact, should the remains of the real John Mohune's body lie in the old vault, then they must be tossing and turning and attempting to rise, for in reality the Colonel remained a loyal subject of the doomed monarch, rather than the wickedest scion of a wicked family.

John Trenchard (a Mohune family name) encounters Blackbeard in *Moonfleet*'s most famous episode. The date is February 1758. John is in the old church, on the morning after a savage storm prefiguring that of 1824. Seaweed is piled up against the graveyard wall, 'from which came a salt rancid smell like a guillemot's egg'. The church is a large and empty building – so empty that people prefer to huddle together in the chancel rather than sit in the body of the church. During the sermon, the scanty congregation is disturbed by a strange hollow booming, coming from the vault. The vault has been closed for forty years, since the burial of Gerald Mohune, 'who burst a blood-vessel drinking at Weymouth races'. The parson explains that the sound is caused by the flooded coffins banging together beneath their feet, while sexton Ratsey affects to take the situation more seriously, announcing portentously that 'when the Moons move, then Moonfleet mourns'.

Curious about this mystery, John Trenchard returns to the churchyard after school the next day, to see if the Mohunes are still moving. He discovers that he is not alone in the churchyard – a favourite haunt of his – when he glimpses Ratsey and Elzevir, the one with his ear to the church wall, the other with a spy-glass, looking out to sea. John, too, often watches the sea, from the top of an altar-tomb at the graveyard's south-eastern corner, which is 'screened from the wind by a thick clump of yew-trees'. The land has dried out after the winter storms, and the heavy clay is cracking. This erosion has left a gap beneath the tomb, revealing the entrance to a passage: an irresistible invitation to the boy.

John returns again after dark, equipped with one of his Aunt Jane's 'best winter candles' and her tinder-box. He follows the passage which leads down to the vault, where he hopes to find Blackbeard's lost treasure, a massive diamond treacherously stolen from King Charles. Stumbling into the vault, he sees the coffins stacked on 'great bookcases' along the walls, while the centre of the vault is filled with casks. 'I had stumbled on the Mohunes' vault, and found it to be nothing but a cellar of gentlemen of the contraband.'

These were the casks which had caused the booming noises, but different sounds now threaten: John is alarmed to hear the voices and footsteps of men entering the passage. 'I knew beside that contraband-men had a way of sealing prying eyes'. Where can he hide? John sees his chance and conceals himself behind a huge coffin lying alone on the top shelf – the coffin, he is to discover, of Blackbeard himself.

The smuggling men – Elzevir and Ratsey among them – are engaged in lugging a batch of unwieldy kegs down into the vault. John dares not move until their work is over and they depart, leaving the vault as John ruefully observes, 'to the dead men and me'. Crawling out of his hiding-place proves difficult; losing his balance he clutches at the coffin, 'and so I came to the ground in a cloud of dust and splinters; having only got hold of a wisp of seaweed, or a handful of those draggled funeral trappings which were strewn about this place'.

When he relights his candle – quenched when he first heard voices – John discovers to his 'throttling fright' that the brittle handful he is grasping is the long black beard of Colonel John Mohune.

Now almost beyond fear, he searches the opened coffin to find, not a diamond, but a silver locket, which to his disappointment contains only a piece of folded paper covered in quotations from the Psalms. Although he does not realise it, this will eventually lead him to the discovery of the diamond. To John it is only a scrap of paper; he has not found the treasure – and he is trapped in the vault. On leaving, the smugglers have re-sealed the entrance gap and there is no other way out. After two days and nights of terror John's cries are heard and he is rescued by Elzevir, only to be disowned by his aunt for his unexplained absence.

John stays at the 'Why Not?' with the landlord, living as his son. Then unexpectedly Elzevir loses the tenancy of the inn in a bitterly contested candle auction. He announces his intention of leaving Moonfleet for a while, taking John with him. The smugglers are being watched, and no longer dare to use the vault. Elzevir decides to hole out in an abandoned cottage near Worth Matravers. There are caves on the shore close by, where the kegs due to arrive on the French ship *Bonaventure* can be safely stored. But when the chosen afternoon comes, they are forced to start rather earlier than planned, because of an unexpected Gulder tide.

> ...word had come to Elzevir that morning that the tide called the Gulder would serve for the beaching of the *Bonaventure* at three instead of five. 'Tis a strange thing the Gulder, and not even sailors can count closely with it; for on the Dorset coast the tide makes four times a day, twice with the common flow, and twice with the Gulder, and this last being shifty and uncertain as to time, flings out many a sea-reckoning.

'Gulder' is the dialect word for the double tide which affects this part of the Dorset coast. It is scarcely mentioned elsewhere in local literature, but was defined by the tireless William Barnes (antiquarian as well as poet) in his *Glossary of the Dorset Dialect* as 'An intermediate or subsidiary flow of the tide about four hours and a-half after high-water. (Weymouth.)' A more comprehensive explanation is provided by George Atkins who believed it to be 'a sort of backlash from the complex tidal system operating around the Isle of Wight. The tide does not fully ebb and flow for four times in the period as Meade Falkner suggests, but at High Water the tide ebbs only a little and then immediately builds up again, being reinforced by another body of water following closely behind, and remaining at High Water for perhaps two hours. The eventual full ebb is rapid.' More recently, it has been thought to be caused by the movement of water within the narrow confines of the English Channel

Tides are governed by the gravitational pull of the moon – and to a lesser extent by that of the more distant sun – and high (or spring) tides occur when the earth lines up with the moon and sun at New or Full Moon. (There was a new moon on November 20th 1824, just before the exceptionally high tide which accompanied the Great Gale.)

Tide times are difficult to predict precisely; double tides even more so. This unpredicted Gulder tide was perhaps an ill-omen for John Trenchard, who had left his aunt's house for ever, and had thrown in his lot with Elzevir, Ratsey and the rest of the smuggling band

Smuggling was a village activity along the Fleet. Before the early eighteenth century most of the action had taken place in the Dorset ports, particularly in Poole, but when Customs and Excise officers became more ubiquitous, the smugglers were forced to change their practices. Hidden reaches of the coast were soon preferred by the smugglers, who began to work together in gangs. Bribing officials was no longer so effective, so instead the smugglers grew bolder and more violent.

Increasingly, the kegs containing liquor, along with well-wrapped parcels of lace, tobacco and other heavily-taxed products, were dropped offshore in the shallow waters of the lagoon to be retrieved by the 'Moonrakers', who went out on bright nights when the coast was clear of excise men and their spies. Web-footed Portland sea dogs were also used. Smooth as seals, they were trained to recover the barrels of brandy and other spirits floating in the Fleet. Once safely ashore, the goods were carted away inland along the rutted tracks and lanes.

As an unobtrusive, low-lying village close to the beach, with a manor house clear out of sight behind the hill, Fleet was an ideal spot for smuggling. Butterstreet Cove (named after the village's only thoroughfare) is one of the 'hives' or inlets along the coast behind Chesil Beach. The word 'Fleet' comes from Old English *fleot,* meaning 'estuary, inlet, creek', and so can be applied to both village and lagoon.

The records of Dorchester Gaol for the period mention two men from Fleet. They were Joseph Zealy, 'labourer, 1826; smuggling; £100, 10 months' and Thomas Zeally, ' labourer, 1840, 34; smuggling; 6 months'. Smuggling was a risky business – penalties included transportation, or even death – but it could be richly rewarding, if only as a means of eking out an otherwise small income.

In the unattributed poem which prefaces *Moonfleet* – presumably written by the author – Falkner makes plain the dangers of this trade in the voice of the 'bold Preventive man':

We will take this smuggling gang,
And those that fight shall hang
Dingle dangle from the execution tree,
Says the Ganger:
Dingle dangle with the weary moon to see.

Like piracy, smuggling is often romanticised, even though it can be a vicious and greedy business. Kipling's famous poem 'A Smugglers' Song' in *Puck of Pook's Hill* presents the smugglers as 'Gentlemen', and local suppliers of luxury goods: *'Brandy for the Parson,/Baccy for the Clerk,/Laces for a lady, letters for a spy,/And watch the wall, my darling, while the Gentlemen go by!'* Unfortunately, however, the behaviour of the smugglers and revenue men was not usually so orderly or genteel as the poem would suggest.

Although he is well-aware of the shady side of the smuggling trade, in *Moonfleet* Falkner's sympathies lie with the smugglers rather than the revenue men, and he makes convincing characters of them. The ancient families in all of his novels are consistently amoral and unscrupulous, but only in *Moonfleet* does he portray a real family, and only in *Moonfleet* is the family quite so maligned. In comparison with the wicked Blackbeard, his smugglers emerge as heroes, and this seems to have been his intention, – even though he goes on to dedicate the book to 'All the Mohunes/of Fleet and Moonfleet/in agro Dorcestrensi/living or dead'.

Tough-minded, knowledgeable and unsentimental, *Moonfleet* has earned its longevity. Like Stevenson's *Kidnapped*, it has never been out of print. Falkner is an underrated writer, and his biography (1995) is difficult to obtain. But Fleet is still remembered now because of his novel. After the Second World War, the house became known as the Moonfleet Manor Hotel; and there have even been postcards of the 'Why Not?' inn. Fleet has become Moonfleet; the landscape of Falkner's imagination, and a greater monument to the writer than his tomb, shaped like a giant swiss roll, in Burford churchyard, Oxfordshire, where his ashes were interred on his death in 1932.

Fleet House is situated over the hill from East Fleet, and like the original village lies very close to the lagoon. It's thought that Maximilian Mohune built the house in the seventeenth century (though William, Earl of Bedford has also been credited with the building), and a few traces of the original structure survive. When the estate passed by marriage in the eighteenth century into the hands of the Gould family,

Nineteenth century engraving of Fleet House, now called Moonfleet Manor.

the house was remodelled in contemporary style, and grand brick stables, complete with pediment and clock tower, were built in the courtyard.

In Victorian times the house was leased by the Goulds to tenants who included the Pretors from 1851, Henry Goodden (a relative of the Goulds) and Sir Henry Peto, who gave a reading-room (now the local library) to the villages of Fleet and Chickerell. Charles George and his family of Bristol brewers bought the house in 1878 and began another rebuilding, adding a second floor, and enlarging the lodge. The agricultural section of the estate – West Fleet Farm, Sea Barn Farm and Bagwell Farm – was sold at auction by the direction of Mrs A L George in 1920. After the death of Mrs George, Fleet House was acquired in 1931 by Lady Celia Brunel Noble, wife of Sir Saxton Armstrong Noble, a director of Armstrong Whitworth (of which Falkner had been the Chairman) and granddaughter of the famous engineer. A further restoration was carried out by the distinguished architect Edwin Lutyens, who must have been bemused by this hotch potch of a house.

In his autobiography *Life in Noble Houses*, Humphrey Brunel Noble recalled a family visit made to the vault of the old church. To their delight they found that the secret passage was still there, but that the vault itself was blocked. The writer Dorothy Gardiner was among the line of people 'almost like a procession of brass Mohunes', crouching ankle-deep in muddy water. They came to the prosaic conclusion that the tunnel was merely a drain. Wyndham Goodden reluctantly came to the same conclusion in his report of another exploration in 1925.

> It was two feet below the surface of the ground, and easily accessible. The tunnel had solid walls cemented on the inside, almost five feet high and two feet wide and was traceable across the churchyard. The book *Moonfleet* was based on its supposed existence. Mr. Harry Gill [Goodden's tenant] had gone as far as he could down the passage…the legend was that the passage connected with the house used by the smugglers.

The last person to leave a recollection of entering the vault itself was a Charlestown man, who as a boy had watched the crypt being opened in the 1870s. 'There were six coffins inside. The kegs bumping about under the chancel floor had smashed all the coffins to pieces. The parson gathered up the bones and the brass plates and put them in a space in the vault and it was sealed again.'

Passage and crypt remain a tantalising mystery; yet another is the attempted auction of the house in 1934 – according to Humphrey Noble the family continued to live at Fleet House until it was requisitioned in 1939 by the Army, when guns were mounted on the tower. Even if no one was tempted to buy the house at the 1934 sale; the catalogue itself is fascinating in its period detail. There was an original stone fireplace, a profusion of cellars, central heating, ten bedrooms and nine 'secondary or servants' bedrooms'. The house came with full manorial rights, 'if any' (though the Goodden family continued to retain the right to collect shingle and seaweed).

When the Pretors had occupied the house in the mid-nineteenth century there had been an *impluvium*: 'the whole centre of the house was open to the winds of heaven, for the purpose of collecting the rain water which fell into a huge reservoir at the basement'. By 1934 the water was coming 'from a spring, (never known to fail), and pumped by a windmill and a small paraffin engine to a storage tank in a field North of the House'. The catalogue also noted that the septic tank emptied into the sea at ebb tide.

The 'charming Pleasure Grounds' around the house were described too. There were walled gardens (with fig tree), terraced lawns and a Grove on the hill above. There was a boathouse and slipway at the south-west corner, and walls ran out to a small mounded island known as 'Gun Island', once used as a stand for wild fowlers. The walls created a romantic water garden in the lagoon, which has sadly faded away.

The catalogue provides a handy guide, though the major chronicler of the house and grounds was Alfred Pretor, classicist and fellow of St Catharine's College Cambridge. As a child, Pretor (1840–1908) lived in Fleet House with his father Samuel, a retired banker from Sherborne, his mother Frances, his sister and his little brother. In a series of semi-biographical essays contemporary with *Moonfleet*, called *Ronald and I*, Pretor provides portraits of the house and some of the people of Fleet, a place he calls 'Broadwater'. The book is dedicated to 'Mrs. Thomas Hardy who suggested and encouraged the publication of these tales'. Emma Hardy – never the recipient of such a dedication from her husband – was a regular and copious correspondent of Pretor's. While advising Emma on her role as the wife of a famous writer, Pretor still considered himself to be the friend of both parties, asking Hardy to write his epitaph. Hardy obligingly unearthed 'an old one' which said, 'If a madness 'tis to weepe/

For a man that's fall'n asleep,/How much more for that we call/Death – the sweetest sleepe of all!' (How Pretor received this contribution is not recorded.)

Ronald and I opens with a description of the approach to the manor from above, descending by the treeless lane which fell slowly down to house and sea.

> The huge square-set building stands on a level plateau, guarded by a semicircle of hills from every wind that blows, excepting the south-west. The architecture is neither impressive in itself nor characteristic of any given period…On the west it faces the Atlantic, and the lawn, merging in the park, falls rapidly seawards till it meets the natural barrier of the beach.

Chesil Bank offers some protection, and house and grounds have a languid air, with tamarisk bushes and palms growing in the sheltered sunny garden. In his novella of 2007, *On Chesil Beach*, Ian McEwan imagines a hotel which is set in similar surroundings.

> The garden vegetation rose up, sensuous and tropical in its profusion, an effect heightened by the grey, soft light and a delicate mist drifting in from the sea, whose steady motion of advance and withdrawal made sounds of gentle thunder, then sudden hissing against the pebbles.

The storms that can shatter this idyll are most frequent in November and February, and Alfred Pretor, like his fellow villagers, was able to detect warning signs like the 'crying' sea, or an ominous sunset 'of war and discord; when colours, the most antagonistic, meet without blending, and produce effects that would be called crude and coarse upon a painter's canvas' against a silvery beach and hills of 'a dark and luminous green'. In the ensuing storm the windows of the house were opaque with brine, and on the roof the tall brick chimneys were rocking in the wind. In yet another storm one chimney crashed through the carriage-house, destroying both the building and the dilapidated coach which was kept there.

The destruction of the coach was something of a relief to the household, as it happened to be a spectral one, with a coachman who was 'a skellington, dressed in black and weepers, for all the world like an undertaker at a funeral'. Like most old houses, Fleet Manor has its share of ghosts (unfortunately omitted from its inventory).

Pretor also relays a creepy little tale told to him by his general factotum, an obliging repository of oral history, who had heard the story from Joseph, the parish clerk, sexton, grave-digger and (with his flageolet) choir-leader. It happened in December 1824, a month after the Great Outrage, when 'visitors by the hundred' arrived, who bring 'their vittles and sit and peant…studin' all the tombstones, and what's writ on 'em – mostly shipwrecks it be, for I doubt if there's half-a-dozen stones in th' old grave-yard but what tells of someone or t'other who was drownded at sea'.

Among the visitors, unexpectedly, is the diocesan Bishop, who is recognisable by his gaiters and his hat 'as shiny as if you'd smoothed it with an iron'. He summons Joseph to attend a burial that evening. Stranger still, it is the funeral of three people, all of whom are to be interred in a single grave.

After dark, Joseph dutifully makes his upward way to the lonely hill settlement of reclusive Farmer Price, where the kitchen door is promptly opened by the Bishop.

> And there right facin' 'em – packed up agin the wall like so many old gran'feyther clocks – stood three coffins, with a piece of glass let in 'em to show the face, and a dead woman in each!
>
> Close handy they were to [Farmer Price] when he took his meals or smoked his pipe; and when he felt a bit lonesome (so he told Joseph) he'd 'go up to 'em and ask 'em how they did, and if they felt comferable. And fresh as peant they were, too: only a bit shriveled, like as 'twere an apple in April.

The burial took place that night in the old churchyard, but the story lingered on, 'told and retold round many a cottage hearth under the quaint but significant title of "Price's Menagerie" '.

For a small place, Fleet had some remarkable clerics. Pretor remembered another priest from his childhood: the village's Rector, Henry John Urquhart, who he commemorates in a story which Pretor claimed was a 'literal study from life'. The Rector's attendance at Sunday services was spasmodic; his congregation waited until the church bell rang before setting out on what could be a fruitless trip. He concealed himself in a 'high square pew' to eat his lunch during the First Lesson, and to smoke a cigar during the

Second. In fine weather, he would often take a short stroll during the service. And for his sermon he used to take up the 'immense' Bible and at his leisure select a text on which to preach.

> The last sermon I ever heard him deliver was on the text "And there shall be no more sea" – an unwise and disquieting subject for a congregation, most of whom came of a race of fishermen, and gained their living from the element which he so confidently annihilated.

In 1879 the *Imperial Gazeteer* stated that the parish of Fleet contained 845 acres of land and 540 acres of water. Almost two-thirds of the parish is water, the cause of the village's existence, and of its destruction. Down by the dark shore, close to where in winter the Fleet stream flows into the lagoon, are the ruins of the destroyed cottages, just visible among the brambles and the reed beds. High above the waters, Butter Street survives lopsidedly. It is much altered, with prominent loft extensions overhanging houses which have lost most of their thatch.

The old church, now a chapel of ease, is open to visitors. The chancel, smaller than the one in the novel, still contains three monuments to the village's ancient land-owners, to Francis, to Maximilian and to Margaret Mohune. Accompanying them is a plaque bearing the coat-of-arms of John Meade Falkner, which was granted to him (and other descendants of his family) in 1905. The shield shows a falcon, 'against a barry nebuly of three argent and vert'. The bird is a pun on Falkner's name; the barry nebuly is a reduced version of the 'six, waving sea-green bars' of *The Nebuly Coat*. Falkner was entitled to a coat of arms, as his branch of the family, including John Meade himself, can be found in *Burke's Landed Gentry*, but it's an odd choice of subject. Is Falkner, a man with a wry sense of humour – mocker of heraldic arms and decaying gentry – having the last laugh here?

The plaque was erected by the Falkner Society in the writer's memory, and beneath the arms is a dedication to the man 'who by his book *Moonfleet* made this place familiar to many'. The village is most remembered for being lost.

*Moonfleet Old Church (*Mick Orr*).*

Bexington-on-Sea

Man is the dream of a shadow

Inscription on a Napier monument in Puncknowle church

Though East Fleet is the most celebrated, there are other half-forgotten lost villages along the shore of Lyme Bay. Chesil Bank shelters a scattering of such places, now shrunken into farmsteads: places like Ashley and Looke with their ruined chapel, Gorwell and Bonvil's Bredy. Modbury, in the Bride valley, has been deserted since as long ago as the Middle Ages.

West Bexington, which lies more directly behind the Chesil, is a village which has been twice abandoned during its lifetime. In the south aisle of the nearby church of St Mary, Puncknowle – an eccentric and charming building stacked with curious monuments – there is a simple plaque, stating that the side chapel was built (or perhaps rebuilt) in about 1660, after the village of West Bexington and its church of St Giles were burnt to the ground by French raiders in 1440. (The lower level of the font is thought to have been salvaged from the remains of the destroyed church.) It was said that any surviving Bexington residents 'were carried away and forced to redeem themselves'.

As Ronald Good points out in his *Lost Villages of Dorset*, this story seems rather unconvincing – why would marauders bother to attack so small and insignificant a place? On the other hand – unlike East Fleet – Bexington sits high above the waters, making a tidal wave an unlikely alternative explanation for its destruction. The only other village in Dorset believed to have been a victim of piracy is the equally small West Ringstead, on the far side of Portland. East Fleet remains the only village in the county to have been destroyed by the sea.

Most of the buildings in Bexington today are comparatively recent, constructed during or after the 1930s. The estate was put up for sale in 1920, when the catalogue hinted at its potential for development as 'a residential estate'. A A Moon in his notes on the village reveals the extent of its shift in that direction by 1931, when Mrs E Duckett had become proprietor of the 'Bexington Manor Guest House', Messrs Perry & Evans advertised themselves as builders and there were two tobacconists. Four years later it was becoming still more commercial. By then, Ernest Callini had established the 'Beach Café' at 'Bexington on Sea' and Geoffrey Norman was proprietor of the 'Fourez' boarding house.

In September 1934 a catalogue was produced for a further sale of the 400 acre Chesil Beach Estate at Bexington-on-Sea. The foreword explained cheerily that 'During the past year Bexington has leapt into prominence as a week-end and summer holiday resort and there can be little doubt that it is going to be in great favour within a year or so'. As well as the existing 'Old World Manor House', the Bexington-on-Sea Estate included '12 Bungalows and Houses, Cafe, Timber

Built Office, Swimming Pool (with Office and 36 Cubicles), Tennis Court, and 24 Summer Bungalows' [two-roomed beach huts].

The design was somewhat military: typical of the ordered nature of early holiday camps, and a shock to the landscape. Until this development, there had been only a rough track down from the ridge to the shore, where it joined the path along the beach. Now the track had become a road, flanked by the permanent brick bungalows: 'Considerable work on roads has been done, and attention is called to the spacious lay-out of suggested roads as indicated on the Plan.' Dead-end roads shot out north, east and west across the diagram and, had they been developed, a whole stretch of wild coastland with its rushes, pools and flowers, would have been lost forever.

Accommodation at the resort was fairly basic. There were only three free-standing lavatory blocks with basins for the twenty-four huts, and no communal provision for bad weather. As extended holidays would have been a new experience for many of the visitors, they were unlikely to have been over-fussy, and the prospectus claimed that the resort was fully booked for the 1934 season.

Whether or not this claim was true, the estate failed to be sold at auction, and the project was abandoned. There had been a proposal to extend the Abbotsbury railway to West Bay and beyond, via Bexington. However, the existing line never proved successful, carrying not – as hoped – iron ore, but mainly unprofitable passengers. Had the plan succeeded, the would-be resort's fate might have been different, though it's doubtful how it could ever have competed with Weymouth, a resort with safe bathing, expansive sands and traditional entertainments, as well as a large railway station.

The estate failed, but the damage was done. Bungalows continue to define the area, both down along the beach road, and up along to Swyre. Two of the plan's permanent bungalows, remnants of the failed scheme, can be distinguished among the grander, more recent additions. The Blue Anchor beach café is still active, having been recently upgraded to become the Club House restaurant; traces of the tennis court can be seen beneath the brambles, and the car park spills out across the pebbles. On the eastern side of the beach is a surviving parade of huts, traditionally shaped, with one oversized intruder in its midst. The shore is regularly lined with fishermen, in their silent and solitary devotions.

Up on the road to Swyre, the houses have an enterprising air. On the corner is Tamarisk Farm (once a group of labourers' cottages) with its organic vegetable shop, while Sea Spring Seeds produces chillies, including the red-hot Dorset Naga. For years now the old manor, with its luxuriant gardens, has been put to use as an inn.

And westwards, along the coastal path – where the holiday houses would have reached – there is a secretive nature reserve of reed beds, and wet meadows, sea kale and yellow horned poppies, lushly undisturbed by the threat of any further development.

At least one person would have watched the growth of Bexington-on-Sea with great dismay. He was the writer H M Tomlinson, who in 1931 had submitted plans for a thatched cottage on Tulk's Hill, two hundred feet above East Bexington, between the heights of Abbotsbury Castle

Detail of the plan for the new house on Tulk's Hill, 1931.

and the sea beneath. In an article in the *Countryman* magazine Tomlinson described the completed house, which was built on a ridge selected for its views and for the wild loneliness of the site. The house's only companions were two round barrows on the hill's summit, claimed by the writer to be the graves of a Mr and Mrs Tulk.

The house was called *Gallion's Reach,* the title of one of Tomlinson's most successful books. (This is a stretch of the Thames in east London, rather than a misspelling.) Built of brick and local forest marble and thatched with reed, the building faced south-west, into the weather, 'with nothing between us and the Bermudas except the occasional trail of a steamer's smoke'.

The house was thoughtfully planned, the garden less so. No attention had been paid to the problems of the gradient or of the rough earth. Not for nothing was the neighbouring farm called 'Labour-in-Vain'. Worse still were the rabbits, undeterred by wire netting and regularly munching their way through the vegetables. 'At least', Tomlinson concluded, 'the cottage has taught us that the land is a problem, older than history, and that only those whose hands are habitually stained by it know anything about it worth attention.'

In 1940 a bomb fell on Tulk's Hill and 'the house made an effort to go, but changed its mind'. Within a year the crater was overgrown with weeds. Water – 'a bright eye' – gathered at the bottom, and around it were scattered 'fossils of the Lias...shells of a sea which flowed here aeons before the earth was ready for us'. The building did survive the war, and still stands, one thatched eyebrow raised at the modern improvements it has endured. Sadly, Tomlinson's many writings have not survived so well.

Henry Major Tomlinson (1873 –1958) came from a seafaring family. His childhood was spent in Poplar; his father worked at the West India Dock. He had a London Board School education and was a promising pupil, but was forced to abandon his schooling after the death of his father, and to take a job with a shipping company. He found himself work as a journalist on the *Morning Leader* and was sent to cover stories at sea. His first book, *The Sea and the Jungle*, (1912) which came out of these experiences, remains his most famous. It is the account of a tramp steamer's voyage from South Wales to the Brazils.

During the First World War Tomlinson worked in France as a war correspondent, then in 1917, sickened by what he had witnessed, he joined H W Massingham on the *Nation*, a paper which was opposed to the conflict.

Before moving to his Tulk's Hill house, Tomlinson had lived in one of the old coastguard cottages on the Abbotsbury shore. The cottages were almost exactly one hundred years old. Their building had begun, as part of a national scheme to counter smuggling, in November 1822 – much to the dismay of the landowner, the third Earl of Ilchester, who was expecting a single boat and watch house to be erected on the site. It was, he wrote in protest to the Prime Minister, Lord Liverpool, both 'annoying and unpleasant', to see five or six cottages appearing as well. They were much too close to his castle. 'I must beg leave,' he continued, 'to state also that it has heretofore been a favourite walk of the family to a piece of water near the situation of the cottages, the privacy of which can no longer exist.' He claimed that building work might also disturb the birds in his Swannery and duck decoy, but made no mention of the fact that in 1791 his father had already erected a 'neat' bathing-house on the beach, complete with a dressing-room and hot and cold water. (Part of a Gothic window-frame from this structure, dated 1791, has ended up in Abbotsbury churchyard.)

Ilchester asked for the cottages to be removed to the eastern end of his property. He had his way, and the terrace was erected instead on the boundary of Abbotsbury and East Bexington, well away from Strangways Castle.

The cottages were sold off in 1924. The Old Coastguards comprised an Officer's House, 'three roomy cottages' and a walled garden. There was, too, a 'Rocket House', a weather-boarded structure with a lead roof and outbuildings. Their purchase offered 'perfect quietude and magnificent sweeping views'. The cottages were bought by the writer and literary critic John Middleton Murry who had been told about Chesil Bank by Thomas Hardy, while Murry was on a visit to Hardy's home at Max Gate. The old man had welcomed him and his companion Violet Le Maistre, the woman who was soon to become Murry's second wife. 'Certainly call upon us in the car', he wrote, 'when you come this way.' Hardy was still smarting from a bitter personal attack made on him by the author George Moore in his book of essays *Conversations in Ebury Street*. Murry had swiftly come to Hardy's defence in the *Adelphi* of April 1924, but like most writers, the old man never forgave any criticism of his work. On his deathbed four years later Hardy dictated a bitter epitaph for his enemy, entitled 'On one who thought no other could write such English as himself'.

'No mortal man beneath the sky
Can write such English as can I
They say it holds no thought my own
What then, such beauty (perfection) is not known.'

Heap dustbins on him:
They'll not meet
The apex of his self conceit.

The manuscript of this unforgiving document, in Florence's Hardy's handwriting, is preserved with its envelope in the archive at Dorset County Museum (together with a second polemic on another of his critics, G K Chesterton).

It was a curious opening for a curious episode in Murry's life. He and Violet moved into the long low terrace with its slate roof, grey as the sea on a stormy day. There was plenty of room, and the building divided naturally into four parts. H M Tomlinson and his wife had one section and the aspiring writer John Stewart Collis had another. Murry's 'A Prologue to Keats' was published in the *Adelphi* in November 1924 and his book about Keats and Shakespeare the following year. John Stewart Collis's first book, on George Bernard Shaw, was published in 1925. Tomlinson had three books (including *Gallion's Reach*) published within the next three years. Living was cheap, and the setting was both lonely and dramatic: ideal for this small community of friends and writers.

The cottage cost Murry £925 at auction, which was considerably more than he had expected to pay. Very fortunately, out of the blue he received a cheque for the enormous sum of £1,000, in royalties from the books of his late wife, the short story writer Katherine Mansfield, who had died of tuberculosis in January 1923. Despite the tormented intensity of their relationship, in Murry's eyes she was the perfect woman. Reflecting in 1935 on their life together he wrote, 'She was a woman simple and lovely in all her ways. I do not think it ever entered my head, at any time, to criticise her in any way.'

This paragon was a hard act to follow, but Violet Le Maistre was a conscientious understudy. Late in 1923 she had approached Murry, the highly-regarded editor of the *Adelphi* magazine, with some of her own short stories. Impressed, Murry invited her to supper to discuss them, though this was not the only reason for his invitation. He had her in mind as a suitable prospective partner for his brother Richard. But during the evening Violet revealed the truth that it was Murry she loved, and not his brother. Like

Katherine before her, she successfully seduced him.

Violet resembled Katherine in appearance. She adopted the same neat bob and fringe, dressed in a similar way and even copied her rival's handwriting. This seems to have struck everyone who visited the Old Coastguards – everyone, that is, except for Murry himself.

While the couple were living in Abbotsbury, Violet became pregnant. Murry was delighted; he had always wanted children of his own, and Katherine had been unable to have them. She and Murry had dreamed of having a boy and a girl, but to his amazement he found that his new wife was utterly distraught on finding that she was to bear a child. While most women would have rejoiced at succeeding where their predecessor had failed, Violet was in despair. She believed

Violet Le Maistre, Katherine Mansfield look-alike.

that Murry would no longer love her if her life deviated in any way from Katherine's.

> 'I don't really want this baby. I've tried to want it but I can't. I only want you. And I am afraid it will come between us. You won't love me so much. You will love her – I know you will.'

She was almost right. When the baby– a girl called Katherine – was born, Violet rejected her. So for four months Murry was obliged to devote all his attention to his daughter, who was a sickly child. When he had nursed her into a state of health he turned back to his wife, and by some 'miracle' Violet accepted her baby.

An Abbotsbury Baby, c.1890, by an unknown photographer.

Katherine was christened in St Nicholas Church, Abbotsbury (where H M Tomlinson was to be buried). The godparents were Thomas and Florence Hardy, who both doted on the child. Murry later recalled how on one of his visits Hardy had made a handkerchief rabbit to entertain his godchild, a trick he surely remembered from his own childhood.

Their happiness was not to last for long. In 1926 Violet gave birth to a second child, a boy named after his father but usually called 'Colin', who himself became famous as the writer 'Richard Cowper'. A third pregnancy was terminated due to the state of Violet's health – like Katherine Mansfield before her, she was diagnosed with tuberculosis.

In 1935 Murry wrote,

> I was completely prepared to tell Violet the bad news, which I did. But I was completely unprepared for her reply. 'O I'm so *glad*!' she said. 'I wanted this to happen.' I stared into her shining eyes. 'You wanted this to happen', I repeated, slowly and dully, while my world turned upside down. 'You see, Golly!' she explained, 'I wanted you to love me as much as you loved Katherine – and how could you, without this?'

Violet was sent to a sanatorium, but they could not help her, and she returned to Abbotsbury for a winter of timeless isolation, one which was recorded by Murry. Often, the family's only visitor of the day was their moustachioed postman.

> 'The Atlantic breakers pounded incessantly against the beach at the bottom of the tamarisk garden, and a faint

> tremor seemed to shake the earth and the long low house continuously. But for the rest, I remember little, save the sense that we were totally withdrawn from the world – a tiny little community.

Murry sold the Old Coastguards in 1928; Violet died in 1930, ending a second turbulent marriage. Murry, it must be said, was not particularly well-equipped to handle this turmoil. Urged on by his ambitious father, he – like his friend H M Tomlinson, whom he met when they both were working for the *Nation* – had been a board school boy. Murry, who learnt to read by the age of two, won one of the first scholarships to Christ's Hospital, and another to Brasenose College, Oxford. His early life was defined by academic work, which equipped him for his future editorships of – most notably – the *Athenaeum* and the *Adelphi*, but less usefully for his emotional life. Tomlinson seems to have been similarly affected: according to John Stewart Collis he admitted to being ignorant about women, and addressed his wife as 'Mums' (though Collis too had what might be called an irregular relationship with his own first wife).

John Stewart Collis had met Murry in about 1923 – not long before they became neighbours – while Murry was working in the British Library on his book *Keats and Shakespeare*. Collis spent just over a year in Abbotsbury, his first glimpse of the county where he was to be employed as a farm labourer, doing forestry work for Rolf Gardiner at his Springhead estate at Fontmell Magna, on Cranborne Chase. Mainly, though, he laboured for a Mr Hannam, who farmed at nearby Tarrant Gunville. Collis's experiences formed the subject of his two most famous books, *While Following the Plough* and *Down to Earth*.

Collis loved the landscape of the Chesil. 'I was born by the sea,' he wrote, 'but never before had seen such light on the horizon', even on the bleakest winter days. He watched the sea in all its seasons, seeing the swans from Abbotsbury fly past 'skimming the waves, heads thrust forward, legs tucked away, and wings making a loud swishing noise. [Then] there were the heat-wave days with the liquid glass lip-lapping on the pebbles'. He swam in the treacherous sea waters when 'the shelving was terribly steep and immediate, and the back-wash overpowering'. Best of all for him were the storms and the occasional tempest, rendering the countryside unrecognisable.

For both Collis and Tomlinson, Dorset was to become home, but after leaving in 1928, Murry did not return. More than the landscape, the chief appeal for him seems to have been the proximity of Thomas Hardy at Max Gate, some ten miles from Abbotsbury. Hardy died early in the year that Murry left the county.

All three writers revered him. While living in the Old Coastguards Collis explored the Wessex of his novels, using Harper's *Hardy Country* as his guide. In his essay 'The Brown Owl', Tomlinson described how his pet bird Joey made the acquaintance of the old man on one of his visits, and on January 12th 1928, the day of Hardy's death, Tomlinson began a monograph about the great author, and cherished hopes of becoming his biographer.

For Murry, though, there were two authors who inspired him above all others: his first wife Katherine Mansfield – and

David Herbert Lawrence. D H Lawrence and Murry first met in 1913 when Lawrence had hopes of publishing a story in *Rhythm*, the first magazine edited by Murry. Murry was greatly inspired by Lawrence's restless creativity and his physicality, and the two men and their partners (neither couple was married) became friends. The friendship was often fractured by quarrels and Lawrence – who rather than biting the hand that fed him, was more likely to rip it off – viciously attacked Murry and Mansfield in his letters. He also portrayed the pair unflatteringly as Gerald and Gudrun in his novel *Women in Love*. After a reconciliation, Lawrence invited Murry (by then a widower) to join himself and Frieda in a community in New Mexico – but this plan came to nothing. When the couple left they were accompanied only by the painter Dorothy Brett, while Murry moved instead to Abbotsbury.

In his autobiography *Between Two Worlds,* 1935, Murry puzzled over the hostility he unwittingly aroused in his fellow-writers: 'There is more than one portrait of myself lurking in the pages of contemporary literature...All alike are hostile: which is significant.' He mentions the 'various attempts made by Lawrence' and 'the distinctly pointed one by Aldous Huxley'. Murry is caricatured as the critic Denis Burlap in Huxley's *Point Counter Point*, 1928, perhaps the most unpleasant character in a novel full of monsters. Like Murry, Huxley admired Lawrence, who (as the writer Mark Rampion) emerges as well as anyone from the book.

*

Coincidentally, just a little further eastward along Chesil Beach was another person much admired by Huxley: in this case for her spiritual qualities. She was an elderly woman called Adela Curtis, leader of the White Ladies of Burton Bradstock, whom Huxley described in *The Perennial Philosophy* (1946) as 'the one living mystic in England'.

Born in Japan in 1864, Adela Marion Curtis was the daughter of a Welsh mother and a hotel builder of fluctuating fortunes. On a visit to England at the age of five she had her first religious experience, when she became aware of the presence of God during a mass adult baptism service at a chapel in Southampton.

Back in England as an adult, she ran a vegetarian restaurant and bookshop in Kensington. Well-educated and handsome, she attended lectures in London by many eminent speakers who later became friends (some of them visited her in Burton Bradstock). From 1904 she began to publish her personal writings – in the form of leaflets, pamphlets and books on spiritual matters. (Dorset History Centre holds over eighty of her works, and even that collection is by no means complete.)

Curtis seems to have first come to prominence in 1907 with her lectures on *The New Mysticism*, published under the pseudonym 'Maranatha', which means 'Come, Lord!' The author was described as being Warden-General of the School of Mysticism, which was then based at 7 Ladbroke Road, London W1. Although always a Christian, her experiences in Asia had drawn her towards Indian mysticism. (Her story *Janârdana*, 1905, tells of a Hindu princess's devotion to her eponymous guru.)

Curtis argued that those who wanted to change the world must first change their own consciousness, which could be done in silence through meditation. In 1912 she bought a country house set among pine woods at Cold Ash, near Newbury in Berkshire, and established an Order of Silence. There was a school, and a self-sufficient farm. This female community was celibate, vegetarian and contemplative. Members did not belong to any particular sect.

The community broke up in 1921 when the exhausted Adela Curtis came to stay in Burton Bradstock with her two nieces, Phyllis and Eve, at what is now Girt House. She must have been a charismatic figure, as so many of her followers joined her that another community was formed in the village. Curtis bought seventeen acres of rough ground, dense with gorse and blackberries, above Burton Mere, from the Pitt-Rivers estate. In 1928 she built the seven-bedroom St Bride's Farm. The prospectus for the community in 1930 explained its origins:

> In 1921 a Bible student bought seventeen acres of derelict farmland on the Dorset sea coast which for fifty years had produced nothing but gorse, brambles and couch grass, rabbits, weasels, stoats, snakes, foxes, badgers and wild birds. The pioneer's purpose was to prove on a small scale that England could not only be self–supporting in food, clothing, fuel, housing, and all other vital necessities, but could provide for a far larger, healthier and happier home population than she had ever have imagined possible, if she would learn the Law of the Lord of the Land. The Bible was taken as the source of inspiration on every subject, and the results were so good that a little colony of wooden

> cottages with quarter-acre fruit and vegetable gardens gradually grew up.

By 1935, when Curtis was again the warden, the colony had become the Christian Contemplatives' Charity, with celibacy as its standard: 'True Celibacy, as in the Supreme Example of Jesus Himself, is True Marriage', Curtis wrote in *The Divine Law of Marriage*, 1934. (Childbirth she dismissed as 'a self-inflicted chastisement'.)

Life was simple, as prescribed in her manual *In Praise of Littleness*, which she had first published in 1919. Although over a century old, the book has a modern ring. Lucid, detailed and written with the benefit of experience, it also gives a sense of how the community worked.

Each woman had a separate wooden hut, not without comfort in the way of bedding. There was little need to cook (and no electricity or mains water). Raw food: home-grown nuts such as walnuts, cobs, hazels and almonds, along with fruit and vegetables from their own quarter-acre patches, would provide a healthier, easier diet. As for clothes, since most shop-bought garments were produced under harsh conditions in factories, the sisters made their own. At first they had a flock of sheep; later they bought in the wool for their looms. Curtis described the processes of flax-growing and weaving in her writings, but advocated the use of silk, produced from hand-reared silk-worms. The sisters wore flowing whitish robes made of flax or silk, which gave them their local name, the White Ladies. (Though Curtis advised wearing nothing at all while swimming.) Her regime was a strict one: she was once observed beating some of the sisters with an umbrella.

Work was worship, but more direct worship was observed seven times a day – at 5 am, 6 am, 9 am, 12 pm, 3 pm, 6 pm and 8 pm, sustained between services with herb drinks and nuts. In 1938 a chapel of Portland stone seating 100 people was added to the buildings under Adela's direction. Over 200 local people attended the dedication service.

By the time of the Second World War, Adela Curtis was well into her seventies, but showed no loss of her formidable energy. In fact the war seemed to give her a new lease of life. She wrote fewer books on meditation, with their close reference to Biblical texts, instead producing more practical handbooks. *The Compost Heap* (1939) for example, gives elaborate and pungent details of the methods of composting, including the use of night soil, collected in 'lavatory pails', which to her mind was 'an intelligent and wholesome system', far superior to more modern methods of collection. Nothing was wasted; from the poor scrubby land around them the sisters had created fertile ground in this way. Despite its fervour, much of the pamphlet – like Curtis's book on the simple life – is still of interest today, and can be read in Afterword 2.

With their hours filled with such peaceful occupations as composting, meditation and bee-keeping, it might be thought that the White Ladies would be opposed to the war. This was not so. *Everyman's War*, a product of 1941, had originally been called *The Way of Peace*, but was re-named, for fear that it might be mistaken for 'Pacific Propaganda'. Pacifists were anathema to Curtis; and she banned them from the community, along with Christian Scientists and indoor water closets. *Dynamic Prayer* was the community's chosen weapon for countering Hitler's 'psychic insanity'

> Only as we are both born *and bred* of the Spirit of God can we work at the Central Power–House of Prayer to overcome Hitler and his superhuman master.

For best results the words of the prayers should be chanted three times: 'Adolph Hitler! Adolph Hitler! Adolph Hitler! Hear the Truth!'

While the War went on, though, the energy seemed to drain from the group. The Army commandeered the main building; most of the followers were now quite elderly. Adela Curtis died there in 1960 aged ninety-six, and the Charity Commissioners gifted what was by now 'a ruin in a jungle' to Othona, which had begun as a community of ex-soldiers who held summer camps at Bradwell-on-Sea in the Essex marshes. (The settlement was named after the Roman fort which had once stood on Bradwell's shore .)

> The Othona community was started after the Second World War as a ramshackle collection of tents and Nissan huts, where Christians could meet to talk about reconciliation between enemies, and understanding people with different beliefs.
>
> Ken Worpole, *350 Miles: an Essex Journey*

By 1961 the community was breaking up under the strain of its success: there were too many visitors, and a second site was needed. When warden John Cross came from Bradwell to investigate Burton Bradstock, he found a group of bungalows around the main house, linked by 'tiny trackways'. Each shack was 'vying with the others in its state of decrepitude and all half-hidden in an overgrowth of blackberry, blackthorn and other rapacious species'. There were of course absolutely no mod cons.

Nevertheless, Othona's second centre opened there during 1965, and, with an ecumenical Christian basis, continued Curtis's ideal of the simple life, dedicated to 'human well-being of body, mind and spirit'. (The huts were sold off, and are now expansive bungalows, hidden among the trees.)

Adela Curtis was not buried beside the chapel as she had wished, but was cremated at Weymouth. In the chapel a wall plaque commemorates her life with a quotation from Jeremiah: 'I have loved thee with an everlasting love'. For Curtis, who was both a mystic and a practical woman, the words of the funeral service must have been particularly apt:

> Forasmuch as it hath pleased Almighty God of his great mercy to take unto himself the soul of our dear sister here departed, we therefore commit her body to the ground; earth to earth, ashes to ashes, dust to dust; in sure and certain hope of the Resurrection to eternal life.

Deadman's Bay

A Saturday Moon and a Sunday full
Never did good and never will

Portland rhyme

Chesil Bank ends abruptly at Portland, where the cobbles pile up against the implacable island of stone: Portland is a natural barrier; they can go no further. The Bank begins almost imperceptibly at Burton Bradstock and stretches eastward for some sixteen miles, growing wider and higher as it goes. There are estimated to be about eighty million pebbles, dwindling slowly in size from east to west, until towards the western end they are no more than the size of peas. The story goes that any local ship-wrecked mariner, cast up limply on the Bank, would immediately know where he was by the size of the pebbles beneath his body.

Chesil Bank was formed ten thousand years ago, at the end of the last Ice Age, when rock debris from the hill tops was washed down into the dry and empty bay by the melting ice, eventually filling the entire basin. Continually tossed about, the debris was driven back to the shore by the force of the waves which swept diagonally across the bay from as far away as Venezuela, shaping and sorting the pebbles as they travelled. The heavier the pebble, the farther it will travel: lighter pebbles drop behind. Chesil Bank, as Paul Nash put it in his Dorset guide, is 'a sea-wall constructed by the sea against itself'. This is one explanation of its formation: there have been many others. A curious structure like this could have been caused by all manner of events. One legend says that the Bank was created overnight, in the aftermath of a furious storm. During that night, as he was being chased by the king's ships, a medieval pirate took refuge from the storm on the Abbotsbury shore. When he awoke the next morning, he found himself safely hidden behind the Bank, with his baffled enemies on the far side of this unexpected obstacle. The Bank's creation has also been attributed to the Devil who, wishing to travel to Portland one day and fearing the cold water, threw a great chain of pebbles across the bay to keep his feet dry.

The large stones at Portland are predominantly flint; other stones are limestone and chert, which is a flint-like material. Further west, as well as decreasing in size, the stones are more varied in type, with red or purple quartzite from Budleigh Salterton, jasper carried by the River Otter, and Cornish granite. There are also a number of exotic strays. The Bank lies on a bed of Kimmeridge clay, and at its greatest height at the Portland end can be about 600 feet wide and stand forty feet above high water. There is an equivalent reach below water on the seaward side, while on the landward side the Bank drops straight down to the lagoon.

In the angle between beach and island lies the village of Chiswell (Chesil, Chesilton or Chessell) which, as the name suggests, has been built straight on to the encroaching shingle. The word chesil means 'pebble'. As Eric Ricketts remarks in his book about Old Portland, 'There are few situations in Britain of such audacity in the siting of buildings against the stupendous forces of nature'. To live in Chiswell is to be continuously aware of the sea and the weather, as stone mason and local poet George Davey well knew.

Ever changing in formation,
Since its very first creation,
Ridges changing in their numbers,
Altered by the giant combers,
With the dragging of a ground swell,
When the East winds to leeward dwell,
In its humour, never silent,
Whether calm or whether violent.
Pebbles on this mighty tier,
Form the music on our ear,
By the notes we can decide,
Patterned by the restless tide.
Whether delicately rippling,
Or with seas annihilating,
Strong this pebbled bank of stone,
Guards our home in Chesil Town

According to Davey, people sometimes even lived – recklessly or desperately – right on the beach. He remembered a man called Dickie Frampton who made his home 'on Chesil shore' around 1900. Fish and firewood came from the sea; his house was simply an upturned boat, the doorway covered 'by remnants of a sail'.

This fishing-place, once the largest village on Portland, has suffered greatly from storms throughout its long history, and was often the target of pirates. Such events were a part of life there; and while little could be done about the raids, various measures were taken to alleviate the damage from the sea. The wide 'opes' (openings) which led up to the overhanging bank of pebbles, also acted as drainage passages for the flood waters. Among the opes in the 1880s were Big Ope, Dark Ope and Little Ope. Big Ope remains intact, and leads up to the Cove House Inn, and Little Ope too (now renamed Lerret Ope) is still in existence. Dark Ope, so-called because it ran under the first floor of a house, has disappeared with the house's demolition. New additions include 'Last Ope' and 'No Ope'. The opes allowed the sea to flow over the streets, often flooding the lower floors of the buildings, going in through the front door and out through the back. As a result, houses were built at higher and higher levels, to minimise the damage. (Ironically enough, the village was short of fresh water, which was supplied by a pump in the middle of the houses, set on a large stone plinth. A bright blue flower-holder marks its site.)

Like the village of Fleet, but on a larger scale, Chiswell was badly affected by the Great Gale of 1824, as George Chamberlaine, rector of Wyke Regis, recorded.

> *November 22, 1824*
> In the Evening of this day, which will ever be memorable for the dreadful Catastrophe which caused such destruction along the whole Western Coast of the Kingdom, the village of Chisel was nearly destroyed, twenty-six of the Inhabitants drowned, and upward of

> eighty Houses damaged or washed down by a tremendous Surf which broke over the Chisel Bank, and bore everything away with irresistible violence before it. This awful Visitation was occasioned by a heavy Gale, which, happening at a spring Tide, and commencing from the South South East, increased till eight o'clock, when it blew a most dreadful Hurricane, such as never had been known before in the memory of Man. At nine o'clock a most horrid scene presented itself. The Sea ran down the Streets of Chisel with a sufficient depth of water to float a vessel of a hundred tons burden: and the Wrecks of the Houses, with the furniture of the poor Inhabitants, were every where strewed on the Shore...The Chisel Beach throughout its whole extent was lowered from thirty feet to twenty; and the Saines [Seines] and Boats of the poor Fishermen of Wyke, as well as those of Portland, almost totally destroyed.

The diary of Portlander John Angel gives a touchingly personal list of those of his friends and neighbours who lost their lives.

> Able Attwool's wife and three children / Grace Mitchell / Mr. Dunning and wife / Wallis, one child /Russell's two children / Old Tom Winter / William White, two children / Anor Pearce / Mrs Byatt killed / Richard Best and Stephen Dryer were washed away in the Ferry House at Ferry Bridge/ Sam Fuzard, one child / John Stone, one child / William Handford was killed in bed, the house was brought down upon him/ Shadrach Stone

> died upon the Beach / James Allen, one child / Robert White died a few days later.

Chiswell (again like Fleet), was effectively destroyed by the storm, and some of its houses lay in ruins well into the twentieth century. In Portland Museum there is a mirror with a carved wooden frame, rescued from the bedroom of a cottage in Brandy Row. Across its silvered surface is a tide-mark, showing the height to which the flood rose during the Great Gale. The sea damage was ultimately completed by the activities of the Council, who demolished over one hundred buildings in the years before the Second World War. Ancient and characterful buildings, their cellars convenient for contraband, were condemned and swept away, leaving the main thoroughfare Brandy Row almost unrecognisable.

A child of Chiswell, Kathleen Winter Saunders spent her summer holidays in such a house at 139 Chiswell. The house had two large cellars, out of which led a dark dead-end passage. One day, she and her cousin explored the passage with a torch and discovered that a stone block had been removed from the end wall. While peering through the hole, she wrote, 'we had the shock of our lives. There was earth and pebble floor rooms running under the houses of Aunt Sis May's and Granny Fitzgerald's with open hearth fire places. It was eerie. We got out a bit quick but didn't tell anyone about it then because we knew we would get into trouble...We found you could walk down to the King's Arms on one side and round to Brandy Row on the other'. The attics in Brandy Row had doors leading through to the end cottage, making them a useful bolt-hole for the smugglers.

Violent storms in 1978-9 led to even greater depopulation, a cause of much concern. The Sea Defence Scheme of 1986 brought back confidence to the village: the beach was raised and inceptor drains inserted. The seawalls were curved inward to force the waves to crest along them. Further barriers were created by the use of gabions (pebbles caged in metal boxes).

The scheme is celebrated in sculptural form at West Weares, a high green slope above the sea wall, where Portland sheep once grazed. ('Weare' is a Celtic word, meaning 'wild rough ground'.) The sculptor was John Maine, whose proposal for the scheme became reality with the help of the people of Chiswell

> [It] takes the form of a landscape work, rising in terraces from the coast path. The curved walls will create wave-like patterns, and support undulating platforms of earth, planted with low-growing species. The higher walls will be made from stone found in the upper strata of the quarries (e.g. 'Slat'), and lower walls will be constructed from a sequence of different types, in the descending order of stone layers found naturally (such as 'Roach', 'Whitbed' and 'Basebed'.) Each type of stone will suggest a different method of wall construction.

Portland is a limestone island, and the houses are built (like much of central London) with rock from its numerous quarries. Along the modest promenade of 1965 one outstanding example can be seen: the Cove House Inn, a sturdy eighteenth century structure, and a remarkable survivor. The writer John Cowper Powys (whose ashes were scattered on Chesil Bank below Abbotsbury in 1963) described it as 'composed of huge square blocks of Portland stone; and although a very small edifice – of not more than half-a-dozen rooms all told – it presented itself...in the form of a massive fortress, that might well have defended the Island in ancient times'. In his novel *Weymouth Sands* the inn is called the Sea-Serpent's Head, and is positioned on the cliffs above the village of Weston, reached from 'up the steep ascent, past one massively-built little house after another, whose stone roofs seemed like organic portions of the hillside'.

This would have been a wise move for the inn, as in its non-fictional position the Cove House faces the weather four-square. Before the building of the promenade, it was actually on the beach. As recently as 2014, the inn was hit by waves sixty feet high during storms which affected much of Lyme Bay (including the Abbotsbury Swannery). Storm shutters kept out the water downstairs and one of the landladies of the inn watched the action from an upstairs window. 'I couldn't resist watching it all unfold', she said. 'It was very exciting'. Below the promenade the descent to the beach is usually a gradual one, but after the winter storms there was a drop of about twenty feet. Chesil Beach itself appeared concave and flattened, its seaward terraces had vanished. On the exposed clay of the beach the rusty iron ribs of a wreck protruded, risen from the dead.

Though not usually so dramatically, the contours of the Beach alter with every spring tide. The pebbles are easily shifted by the undertow. But renewal after a great storm can sometimes take years. A note on an old (pre-1839) map offers an explanation of how the process works: 'Beneath the Pebbles is a firm Black Clay which appears when a strong S.E. wind blows. The Bank is then swept from one Part to the other of the stones, and remains only of clay till such time as S.W. wind blows, when the sea throws them up to cover the Bank again.'

In The *Well-Beloved*, his rather bizarre novel set on Portland, Thomas Hardy calls the Chesil coast 'Deadman's Bay'. This may have been its old name – and local shipwreck maps seem to endorse it, as they are clotted and crammed with the names of vessels which have come to grief here in greater numbers than anywhere else around the island or in the bay. The Isle of Portland is surrounded by dangerous waters. On the further side are the conflicting currents of the Race, described by Hutchins as 'a place dangerous to pass in the calmest seasons, owing to the meeting of two tides or setting-in of the currents from the French and English shores, which cause a continual bubbling and rippling of the water, and the foulness and rockyness of the ground, which makes that space of the seabed boil like a pot, and drives vessels on shore on the beach west of the island'. There are, too, the treacherous sandbanks called the Shambles (or Shingles) four miles to the east of the lighthouse at Portland Bill. In Lyme Bay, Hardy wrote, you could hear the warning: the ominous sound of 'a long-drawn rattling, as if of bones between huge canine jaws. It came from the vast concave of Deadman's Bay, rising and falling against the pebble dyke'.

Washed-up, unidentified corpses were frequent finds. They were often naked: 'The sea undresses them', Thomas Hardy was told. It has been remarked that the old church at Fleet was used as a mortuary chapel in the nineteenth century, and in Chiswell too there was a 'Dead House'. This was close to the beach, adjoining the Ranter's Lodge, a former store house where the Primitive Methodists used to meet. Bodies from shipwrecks were taken to the House while awaiting Christian burial. There is a Strangers' Cemetery not far away, above Chiswell. (The shell of a third mortuary house can still be seen in Southover on the seaward side of Burton Bradstock, at the other end of Chesil Bank. Its table, on which bodies were laid out, was made from the hatch of a wrecked schooner, the *Flirt*.)

In later years the lower level of the Dead House was used for storing lobster pots. A driftwood fire burned there, heating a large copper boiler in which the nets were dyed. Upstairs (where doors opened on to the beach) the lerrets – local boats – were repaired and varnished. (Now the house itself has been refurbished and is let, like its neighbour, as an 'artist's studio'.)

Chapels like the Ranter's Lodge were a feature of non-conformist Chiswell. (Portland was said to be made up of 'Stone, Convicts and Methodists'.) There was a Methodist Chapel, an Independent Chapel and the 'Conjurors' Lodge', two of whose leaders, Charles Whittle and Robert Hinde, had been unfairly expelled from their mother chapel on suspicion of witchcraft in 1816. Another nickname for the chapel was 'Bedlam', which was also the title of George Davey's poem about this suspect place.

About the time when Wesley made
An entrance to this Isle.

Flamboyance was a means to make
Impressions here in style.

That storied house resolved to be
Of notice years ago,
Evangelists came here to preach,
To let the people know
The message that the Bible gave
To ev'ryone world wide,
That Christ atoned for mankind's sins
As on the cross he died.

The steps that led to that old house
A rostrum they became
But with the rantings, scorn set in,
Cat-calls made it a game.
The preachers were theatrical
To get their message through,
But all became a comedy
As strong derision grew.

Thus with the roistering goings on
The hullaballoo that came,
'Twas like a mad house in its day,
So Bedlam got its name.

About ten years later, Whittle and Hinde were invited back into the fold, but the building has been left, conspicuous for its external flight of stairs, leading to the upper room where the meetings were held.

Chiswell was also well-supplied with inns, with which the chapels seemed happily to co-exist, although not everyone accepted the juxtaposition. Particularly zealous against the evils of drink was a man by the name of Hiram Otter. He was a massively-built quarryman and Salvation Army convert, who carved a pathway through West Weares to a spot which he christened 'Halleluiah Bay'. As he went, he adorned the white limestone rocks along his way with biblical texts (such as might once have been seen on the stiles and fences of inland Dorset). Thanks to his labours, the cove became a popular bathing-place. The path is still there, under the dark cliffs which are heavy with quarry waste and liable to landslips, and beside the former fishing huts of the Cove. The sea has washed away the scriptures.

Gone too are the lerrets, boats which originated on Portland, but came to be used more extensively along the Chesil. They were said to be the invention of an eighteenth-century Portland sailor who, when visiting Italy, admired the double-prowed Mediterranean boats, and adapted the design for use in Chesil Cove. One of the boats the sailor noticed was called Lady of Loretto – hence the rather less romantic 'lerret'.

These all-purpose vessels were suitable for mackerel fishing, for smuggling and for sea rescue. (Even after a lifeboat was introduced in 1826 Portland men preferred to keep on using lerrets, despite the greater risks involved.) They were also used for shipping stone. The boats were clinker-built and flat-bottomed and it was claimed that they never capsized. They had neither rudder nor sails, and were powered by four to six oarsmen. Extra men were needed to launch and beach the boats because of the bows at each end which allowed them to come and go more easily in rough seas.

Fishing from the beach has greatly declined. One of the last of the fishermen, Ian Stone, is said to have caught a nine foot long shark in his net. He wrestled with the shark rather than cutting it out, to avoid any damage to his net. All kinds of creatures are washed up on the beach, including dolphins, whose deaths must be reported, as they belong to the Queen. At night, anglers still fish along the esplanade in a mysterious ring of light, formerly supplied by Tilley lamps.

A second type of craft, used specifically on the Fleet, was the backwater trow, another double-ended, flat-bottomed boat (and flat-bottomed boats are rare in Britain). Slightly shorter than the lerret, it had a raised seat in the stern for a marksman: trows were used on the lagoon for wild fowling as well as for fishing. When the water was too low for rowing, they were pushed by *quonts*: boat poles forked at their outer ends. (William Barnes was puzzled by the Fleet fishermen's use of this word, and ingeniously suggested that it could have derived from the Latin *contus*, which he said 'means such a shoving pole...which might have come from the monks at Abbotsbury'.)

The lerrets were often involved in sea rescues. All manner of ships have at some time been swept into the Bay and on to the apparent safety of the Chesil by the strength of the currents. Once there, they are trapped between the breakers and the pebbles' friction. At least forty ships have been wrecked along these shores, from the English vessels *John* in 1669 and *Angel Guardian*, 1681, and the French *Pelerin*, 1784, to the ketch *Edwin & Sarah*, 1882, the Norwegian brig *Ora et Labora*, 1891 and the Russian schooner, *Emma Maria* in 1903.

Another wreck, in which men from the Chesil were drowned, happened not in Deadman's Bay, but off the coast of Aberdeenshire in 1881. The ship – like the tavern in John Meade Falkner's *Moonfleet* – was the Bridport-based *Why Not?* which might have suggested to the writer the name for his inn. Falkner was as well-informed about wrecks as he was about smuggling, and the final and most dramatic scene in his novel comes when John Trenchard and Elzevir Block, both experienced sailors, are themselves shipwrecked.

The lives of the two men had not gone well after they left Moonfleet. Accused of stealing Blackbeard's fatal diamond, they were sentenced to the galleys for life and sent as slaves to Ymeguen in Holland, where they were branded on the left cheek with a Y. (Ymeguen, incidentally, does not appear on modern maps of the country.) After ten years hard labour, they were sentenced to more of the same, and were on the way to Java when their brig ran into trouble. The two men realise that they are adrift in Moonfleet Bay.

> ...I could hear the awful roar of the under-tow sucking back the pebbles on to the beach. The last time I could remember hearing that roar was when I lay, as a boy, one summer's night 'twixt sleep and waking, in the little white-washed bedroom at my aunt's; and I wondered now if any sat before their inland hearths this night, and hearing that far distant roar, would throw another log on the fire, and thank God they were not fighting for their lives in Moonfleet Bay.

Falkner describes the storm, the wild high seas and the ship's slow break-up as vividly as an old salt might tell the tale. He describes the rescuers waiting on the shore, wanting to save lives, 'yet anxious not to miss their chance of booty, if Providence should rule that wrecked she must be'. The men were burning a blue light: 'They burn that light in Moonfleet Bay just where a little streak of clay crops out beneath the pebbles, and if a vessel can make that spot she gets a softer bottom. So we put the wheel over a bit, and set her straight for the flare.'

The light in Moonfleet Bay (F R Exell)

The ship's crew have deserted; the other prisoners have taken to the boats, John and Elsevir are alone on the disintegrating vessel. They jump into the waves, and succeed in reaching the rope the rescuers have flung out to them from the shore. Elsevir pushes John towards the safety of this line, but fails to reach it himself. His body is found on the beach the next day.

The Moonfleet men were burning a blue light to help the distressed ship run aground safely, but they were also hopeful of 'booty'. The term 'wrecking' can mean either watching out for and plundering a wreck – or luring a ship on to the rocks by showing a false light or signal. How often the latter happened is uncertain, and it has been argued that a ship would have to be in distress already to be close enough to see the signal.

Undoubtedly, though, wrecks were regularly plundered. Men who had shown immense courage in saving a ship's crew and passengers from the dangerous waters, would then ruthlessly proceed to strip the ship's carcase of all its valuables. This seems to have been regarded as a matter of course. The diary of a Portlander named John Thomas Elliott certainly gives that business-like impression.

> Wind about East fresh wind. A Schooner called the "Judy" of Exeter it appears that she struck first on "Godnor Ledge" and drifted into "Broad Hope", and wrecked there. Her crew were all saved. They were taken off the wreck by John Lawman's boat and went ashore at "Collard". Her crew was saved. Her cargo consisted of coals. We worked up her wreck by the third. In the following January 1868 a Barque called the "Bank" ran on shore a

> few yards from where the "Judy" was wrecked at "Broad Hope". She was about 500 tons. Her cargo was coals and coke, railroad iron and fire brick. Her crew was saved. We worked on board and stripped her for 8 shillings – the hull was sold, and bought by John Way.

The *Hope* (or *Hoop*) of Amsterdam, lost off Fleet in 1748, was carrying perhaps the most valuable cargo of any Lyme Bay wreck. According to Hutchins's *History*, she ran aground at one or two in the morning on January 16th, because there was 'no light from the Portland lighthouses either by reason of the great mist, or the neglect of persons concerned there'. On impact, 'the mast fell with the shock', enabling the crew to clamber ashore. A mob immediately formed (of 3,000 or 4,000 men, according to Hutchins) who spent ten days digging for the ship's treasure of gold bullion, silver and jewels.

> The shore was a scene of unheard-of riot, violence and barbarity; and it is surprising that no one was killed. But as the weather was about this time extremely cold and windy some perished on the beach. The popular pleas for this rapine were, that the Dutch were pirates...they imagined it lawful to plunder pirates.

In 1872 during a gale the *Royal Adelaide*, an iron-built merchant ship, rolled broadside on to Chesil Bank, between the Cove and Wyke Regis. She was carrying a grocer's shop of a cargo, including rum, gin and cotton, sugar and paper. There were also live animals – pigs, dogs and horses – and thirty-nine emigrants bound for Australia. Nine people were drowned (and all of the livestock except for one pig). Crowds of people descended on the wreck, drinking the liquor and salvaging all they could of the rest of the cargo. Four people died of drunkenness and the cold. (This shameful episode was the last of its kind in Portland's history.)

The wreck of the *Adelaide* still lies on the seabed, and is popular with divers, searching for a different sort of treasure. In summer, rare grey triggerfish swim amongst the wreckage. The Chesil Beach Watch monitors conditions both under the sea and on the shore in the Cove, noting any changes, and taking action against pollution, particularly that caused by 'ghost' fishing gear: the nets and lines left behind or discarded by vessels, most of them commercial ones.

After the winter storms of 2014, the Cove's beach was more than once dishevelled by heaps of debris: driftwood, a palm tree, fish-netting, the bodies of a dolphin and a cow, crates, tubs of chemicals and other brightly-coloured and indestructible pieces of plastic. Some of this unsightly mass must have travelled thousands of miles. Within days of the storms, the people of Portland had cleared the shoreline of every scrap: a very different kind of salvaging from that of the *Adelaide*.

*

All Saints with St Edmund, the parish church of Wyke Regis, sits on the side of a hill, its tower just visible above the surrounding trees and newer development, and bounded by busy roads. It is a fourteenth-century building, expansive and airy. The church has three burial grounds, necessary partly because it was once the mother church of Weymouth, but also because it was the church closest to Deadman's Bay. As John Cowper Powys described them, the grounds are 'crowded thick with the bones of wrecked men – most of them anonymous and buried together under the name of the vessel that carried them down...' Here, a single grave contains 140 of the passengers and crew of the *Alexander*, an East Indiaman wrecked in the Bay in 1815. In the older churchyard the inscriptions on the graves have mostly weathered into illegibility, though one, dangerously close to the road, can be partially deciphered:

> Sacred to the memory of William Lewis
> Who was killed by a shot from the "Pygmy" schooner
> 21st March 1822 aged 33 years

This, and the epitaph that follows, were adopted by John Meade Falkner for his own purposes in the opening scene of *Moonfleet*. As well as having a similar inscription, David Block's stone carries the same headpiece as William Lewis's – 'a little sea-piece carved at the top of the stone, which showed a schooner boarding a cutter'. Falkner must have spent hours looking at the Wyke tombstones to find this particular memorial.

Away from coast, in the centre of Portland, there is another heavily impressive graveyard around the parish church of St George Reforne, with stones commemorating some of the Chesil dead. Many of the graves have been carved by masons using very local stone, producing not off-the-peg designs, but their own, often fanciful creations: a glorious company of angels rise from this burial ground.

The churchyard's inhabitants often died violent deaths, including four Chiswell people killed by a press gang in 1803. Press gangs had appeared on Portland in the 1630s, at a time when the quarrymen were mining stone for the new St Paul's Cathedral. To prevent this practice, Portland quarrymen and sailors were exempted from impression. This, however, did not stop Captain George Wolfe from attempting to impress Chiswell men in 1803. During the fracas that followed three local men were killed, and Mary Way, aged 21 was wounded by musket bullets. A plaque in the church records this event:

> To the memory of the following islanders
> Who were shot by the Press Gang.
> During its unlawful raid on the Royal Manor of Portland
> In what was known as the Easton Massacre.
> On April 2nd1803.
> Alexander Andrews Quarryman.
> Richard Flann Quarryman.
> William Lano Blacksmith.
> And Mary Way who died later of
> Wounds received in the same raid.

Mary Way died seven weeks later on May 21st. She and her father have tombstones side by side in St George's churchyard.

Other stones record further tragedies. Fifty-one victims of the Great Gale were buried there. Among them was William Hansford, aged 61, one of those listed as having died in Chiswell : 'his Leg was broken in attempting to make his escape afterwards the House fell on him'. Another grave contains the bodies of two young girls whose epitaph reads

Nipt in the buds by wind and storm
And by the mighty raging sea
Torn from their parents tender arms
Children that were their parents joy

Carpenter Jamieson is buried with five other, unknown mariners, drowned in 1877 when his ship the *Avalanche* tried and failed to land in Chesil Cove, after colliding with the *Forest* off Portland Bill. (So great was the loss of life in this shipwreck that St Andrew's Church in Southwell was built as a memorial. It is widely known as the 'Avalanche Church'.) Here also lies an assistant prison warden murdered by a convict, a man killed by lightning, and a casualty of the *Lusitania*. The violent nature of so many of the deaths – and the elaborate monuments which record them – make the churchyard of St George Reforne a splendidly grim place, rising high over the treacherous Deadman's Bay where so many of the departed met their end.

*

On a fine day, the clarity of the light on the island is dazzling. The weather is temperamental: not for nothing is Portland among the roll call of names in the daily shipping forecast. The sea can change from slate to silver in an instant. Yet although other scenic fishing villages became artists' colonies in *fin de siècle* England – places like Newlyn, Staithes, Walberswick and, later, St Ives – this didn't happen in Chiswell, perhaps because of the dilapidated state of the housing at that time. Many of the cottages were still in ruins from the Great Gale; others were sliding into the sea.

In 1934 John Piper, an artist who loved the ramshackle and ruinous, went to stay in Abbotsbury with his future wife Myfanwy Evans. They walked the tortuous length of Chesil Bank, and Piper made a pen and ink sketch of a figure reclining uncomfortably on the shingle (a rare example of a peopled landscape in his work). On Portland he drew and painted the scattered slabs of stone around the quarries and the dreamily chaotic landscapes of the Bill. He painted St George Reforne church and gravestones in their weather-beaten grandeur, over and over again.

Paul Nash, too, visited Portland in the thirties. He was impressed by the great boulders to be found everywhere on cliffs and shore and in the quarries. Using a red filter, which had the effect of dramatically darkening the sky, he photographed the stones and, from Priory Corner above Chiswell, the long ragged line of Chesil Bank. He photographed a massive wreck, helpless as a beached whale upon the shoreline. His images are impressions of the island's strength.

Another regular visitor was Richard Eurich. Born in Bradford in 1903, as a young man he used to stay with his cousins in Weymouth, where his uncle ran a printer's shop. Many of his paintings were of the resort, but he also explored the then little-visited length of Chesil Bank, which became important to his development as a painter. In his book on Dorset artists, Paul Davies noted that 'painting in so exposed a place posed inevitable practical problems for the outdoor painter, who was soon forced to rely on quick pencil sketches made on the spot which were later elaborated and worked up with the use of an acute memory. This created the characteristically accurate and detailed atmosphere of

[Eurich's] coastal landscape…' Eurich worked as a war artist for the Admiralty during the Second World War, a role for which he was already well-adapted.

There was one painter 'of picturesque scenes' who ventured to invest in Chiswell property. George Carline's hobby was buying houses, and around 1900 he bought four of them in the village. It was fortunate that the houses were cheap, as two of them were soon swept away. The other two survive, an upright pair on the main street; one of them still belonging to the Carline family. The oldest part of that house dates from the seventeenth century. It is three-storied, and the last resident there, Bob Anthony, (known as 'The Wobbler') kept his lobster pots in the attic. The house was lit by gas then, and had no bathroom.

After Bob Anthony's death in 1985, the Carline family began to use the house as a holiday home. George Carline's daughter-in-law, Nancy Carline, painted in Chiswell during the last twenty years of her life, come spring, come summer. Born in 1909, Nancy attended the Slade School of Art under Henry Tonks and Philip Wilson Steer. For two seasons she assisted in the costume department of the Sadler's Wells Ballet, where she met Vladimir Polunin who with his wife Elizabeth had been the principal set designers for Diaghilev's Ballet Russe. She worked with designs created by Léon Bakst and Picasso. Polunin taught a stage design course at the Slade which Nancy later joined. Wilson Steer had encouraged her to work en plein air; while Polunin taught her how to develop a fresher, freer approach to painting which produced the mood pieces, townscapes and landscapes with figures so characteristic of her work.

During her second period at the Slade Nancy met Richard Carline, youngest of George Carline's five children. (His sister Hilda, another painter, married the artist Stanley Spencer.) They worked and painted together and married in 1950. Nancy exhibited at the New English Art Club and in the Royal Academy's summer shows. When in Chiswell, she would wander across from the house to the beach, where she painted on small, easily-portable panels, sitting on a ledge below the esplanade, sheltered from the wind. She worked outside whenever possible, and afterwards she might round off the day with a 'little gin' from the nearby Cove House inn. Her seascapes are full of light, soft or sharp on sea or shingle. Here there is a boat, and there some of the figures who seem suddenly to appear, at times diminished or part-concealed, by the pebbled wall of Chesil Bank. Her paintings bring colour and intimacy to scenes more usually presented in a conventionally dark and gloomy manner. In 1992 as part of an exhibition at the now sadly-defunct Chesil Gallery in Chiswell, nine of Nancy Carline's paintings were shown on their home ground.

Little is known about another artist, John William Upham, who worked in Weymouth and Portland. He was born in Offwell near Honiton in 1772 and rose to become a Royal Academician, with Princess Augusta, a daughter of George III, as his patron. (The royal family was very fond of holidaying in Weymouth.) Between 1802 and 1805 Upham was commissioned by John Penn, who became a formidable Governor of Portland, to record a set of island scenes. A picture called 'The Commons at Chesilton' shows Penn riding his horse above village and

Beach, while women and children offer to sell him such seaside souvenirs as fossils and shells. Chiswell can be seen in the background, compact and sturdy.

In later life, Upham moved to Weymouth, where he died in 1828. He was buried in Wyke churchyard, and his grave is just a few feet away from that of William Lewis, the mariner whose now-illegible epitaph can still be read in the opening chapter of *Moonfleet.*

Leaving the Island: Ferry Bridge

Portland was once a true island, attached to the mainland by the brittle thread of Chesil Bank. Walking along the mile-long stretch between Chesil Cove and Wyke Regis is like walking in a dream, tread-milling an endless trail, footsteps vanishing back into the shingle. One observer, quoted by Hutchins, recommended walking on the seaward side of the Bank, which was 'by far the firmest and easiest for our horses, especially as the pebbles were somewhat bound together by the marine plants growing in patches along the water side'. Either way, it is hard, slow work.

For centuries, the only other access to the mainland was by ferry, across a short but risky passage at Small Mouth, at the Weymouth end of the Bank. The sea flows through this narrow channel from Portland Harbour to supply the water for the Fleet lagoon, which here at its source is saline and tidal.

Much further along the Bank, diagonally opposite the Bridging Hard in Wyke Regis, is the Bound Stone, which marks the limit of the Royal Manor of Portland. It is the site of the Beating of the Bounds, which occurs on Ascension Day every seventh year. Portland is different from other places along the Fleet, having never been under the control of a great landowner. Instead it was accountable directly to the monarch, without the intervention of any squire or baron. It has been a Royal Manor since Saxon times but, as the monarch seldom visited the island, it was administered by a Steward, while the Reeve collected the rents.

Fleet had its Mohuns, and Wyke Regis, as the name suggests, had been the property of the Crown – but was latterly held 'of the Crown' by the Earls of Ilchester. The manor of Langton Herring passed through many hands including those of the Duchy of Cornwall. At one time it was divided into two sections, the second being known as Ryme Extrinseca, awkwardly paired with the North Dorset village of Ryme Intrinseca, a fair distance away in country miles. The second part of Langton's name came from its early ownership by the Harang family, who also held Chaldon Herring and Winterborne Herringston. The lord of Langton Manor had Right of Wreck and of the fishing and fowling along the Fleet waters, and its eastern and western boundaries were marked by stones placed, like that of Portland, upon the crest of the Chesil Bank.

Major W Sparks, Langton's lord of the manor in 1893, reported that the stones were still in position at that date. The Great Storm of 1824 had displaced them (the breaching of the Bank was thought to have been close to the site of the western boundary stone) but they had been restored in a ceremony witnessed by representatives of the manors of Abbotsbury, Langton Herring and Fleet.

Being an island and under separate distant governance, Portland preserved its customs and way of life for longer than these other places. The open field system was protected by the Manorial Court, which still meets yearly to deal with local issues. Later, this 'Court Leet' became increasingly concerned with quarrying (an industry which offered the islanders the choice of work other than farming or fishing). The Court's powers have been restricted, however, since the passing of the Law of Property Act in 1935.

Portlanders, both men and women, were independent and individual people; Portland women possessed property rights probably unparalleled anywhere in England. They kept themselves to themselves, outsiders – 'kimberlins' – were not welcomed. (The origin of this word is obscure. According to the Oxford English Dictionary, the most likely derivation is from the Middle English word 'kymeling' or 'comeling', meaning 'one who has come to a place, not a permanent resident, an immigrant, newcomer, stranger, sojourner'.)

The inward-turning nature of the Portlanders meant that their particular variant of the Dorset dialect lasted longer than that of other districts. When William Barnes was writing his *Glossary of the Dorset Dialect* in 1863 it was still possible to distinguish native speakers from Sturminster Newton in the north from those of Dorchester in the south. According to Portlander George Davey, broad dialect continued to be spoken around Southwell and the Bill until the outbreak of the Second World War.

In 1979 Portlander Bob Wollage collected a number of Dorset dialect words, most of them not recorded by the Reverend William Barnes. They included *pinion end, zowel stick, gourd, cliffy, taffold or taffle, dern, shen, mingy, scouced, nish, nunk, snob sticks* and – best of all – *cooby*, which means 'a peculiar person'. Further terms, also absent from Barnes's glossary, were contributed by George Davey in 2011 to the *Portland Free News*. The list included *lawn*: 'Portland arable is split into small pieces known as lawn'; *ain't sidden*: 'I haven't seen him' and *hark et will*: 'hark at that seagull'. Other local words – ones more likely to endure – come from the precise vocabulary of the stone masons. Davey mentions *arris*: 'edge of a stone'; *spalls*: 'trimmings from the stone blocks' and *poxed*: 'work that is spoilt'. Not surprisingly, the stone industry's extensive vernacular overlaps with that of the quarries in Purbeck, East Dorset.

Portland people often intermarried: the islanders had only a few surnames between them. J W ('Gaffer') Warren, local historian, noted that there was a time when 90% of the island's population had the surnames of Pearce, Stone, Comben, Attwooll, Flew or White. In addition, only a small number of – mostly Biblical – forenames were used, resulting in an ingenious variety of nicknames. Courting couples followed the practice of not marrying until the girl became pregnant, a practical arrangement much frowned on by some contemporary observers.

The island hasn't altogether changed. With its quarries, prisons, and moody weather, Portland is a tough, working place, an antidote to cream tea Dorset. (Tellingly, it gets short shrift in many of the guidebooks to the county.) But there was one event above all others which noticeably affected the island's character, and that was the building of the ferry bridge.

First mentioned in the thirteenth century, the ferry was simply a boat drawn across the passage by a rope attached to posts at each end. Later a second boat was added for horses and cattle, the other one being used by foot passengers. The idea of a bridge was mooted on several occasions before any action was taken. In a petition to Weymouth visitor George III, the inhabitants explained that the ferry was 'a very dangerous navigation by reason of the strong currents and eddies, as well as the great depth of water'. Crossings were 'intimidating to horses', and sometimes proved fatal to both man and beast.

The catalyst for the building of the bridge was that most destructive of episodes in Lyme Bay: the Great Gale of 1824. The Passage House was swept away, and Richard Best the ferryman was drowned while trying to rescue a horse. The sand bar which could be crossed at low tide also vanished, and the channel itself was so eroded that it became four times wider than before.

After the Great Gale a temporary ferry was erected – a bridge would have been costly, and there were some bureau cratic hurdles. The tolls from the ferry belonged to the monarch, and an Act of Parliament would be required to change this situation. When the Act finally appeared in 1835, it ran to thirty-nine complex pages. Commissioners had to be approved; they must be landowners and worth at least £40 a year. Elaborate toll charges were drawn up – each pig, for instance, was to be charged 2d and each horse or mule 5d. When finally completed, the bridge was 600 feet long and 21 feet wide, and was supported on timber piles which were faced with copper above sea level. It opened for business at the end of January 1839 and proved so popular that it became necessary to strengthen it within ten years. The building of the bridge inevitably brought an end to much of Portland's isolation, and with it many of the old beliefs and customs.

Portland's Fair continued, however (lasting to this day in the form of a funfair). Its traditional date was November 5th, though it long pre-dated the activities of Guy Fawkes. For the annual fair, sheep and pigs would be transported over from the mainland by boat, while the cattle would be forced to swim across the Small Mouth channel.

The day was rounded off with music and dancing in the evening. (At the Sun Inn, Fortuneswell, in 1830, the floor gave way under the weight of the people performing a 'mazey' dance.) By the 1850s the Fair's attractions included amusements as well as the traditional sale of farm animals. Gingerbread, toys and sweetmeats were sold and there was a peepshow. At dusk the Fair spun out of control with exploding fireworks, bonfires, and the jingle-jangle of

Portland Fair in its heyday

organ music.

In 1860, the construction of both Prince Albert's pet project, the Breakwater in Portland Harbour, and of the Verne Citadel, was proceeding fast and furiously, bringing an influx of convicts, prison officers and military personnel. The population swelled from 2852 in 1841 to 8468 in 1861, causing a rapid change in the demographic. Men now far outnumbered women, and there were a great many incomers from the mainland. News of these developments attracted an unusually large number of showmen to the Fair in 1860, some of whom were obliged to camp on land beside Fortuneswell's Wesleyan Chapel. A prayer meeting had to be cancelled, which created a certain amount of outrage. Caravans were moved to a site in Victoria Square, Chiswell, which in 1862 became the permanent setting for the Fair. Cattle continued to be sold separately in Fortuneswell until 1902, when the fair field was closed for good.

In her memoir of Chiswell, Kathleen Winter Saunders wrote that the Fair was a highlight of her young years, despite the fact that it almost always rains on the long-awaited day. The Fair was based at Baker's Ground, but spread around the village. Kathleen remembered the 'Dragons' outside her house in Brandy Row: 'great big lumbering wooden cars with chassis like dragons with the Hurdy Gurdy music grinding out in the centre...It was backed by beautiful decorated glass panels which reflected the silver pipes and it was lovely. Next to that was the Ghost House and the shrieks coming from there made everyone stop to find out what was going on.' Portlander Tom Neilson remembered himself and the other children gathering coins shed by the people on the rides. The Townsend family, who brought with them their famous Dodgems, usually stayed for a week

There was a Fat Lady, a hairy Lady, a nougat stall by the Beach Inn and a Cake walk. The pubs were packed, and outside their doors the cheapskates sold bed-sheets and crockery and gimcrack jewellery. Other side-shows included 'numerous rifle ranges, dart throwing, hoopla, raffles, candy floss and hot-dog stalls' as Ken Saunders recalled in 1991.

According to the *Dorset Evening Echo* (published on the mainland) Portlanders had their own coobyish custom at the fair. They would arrive, wearing raincoats and armed with 'teasers', which looked like long toothpaste tubes. They then spent most of the evening squirting each other with water from the tubes. Barrels of water were provided at each end of the village, so that the teasers could be refilled. (Islanders, however, have no memory of this.)

Not everyone approved of the fair. Bob Wollage, who was a member of the Wesleyan Chapel in Southwell, noted that their annual 'tea meeting, come sports day' was always held on the same day as the fair, to discourage members from attending such an unseemly event. This made for difficult choices, as treats on the island were rare.

In 1887, the span of the wooden bridge was shortened as an economy, but it was evident that a replacement bridge was needed. The engineer of this iron bridge was Sir John Coode, the engineer responsible for the Portland Breakwater. He drew up plans for an iron bridge, which proved unpopular as, inevitably, the Portlanders would have preferred a bridge built of local stone. Although this might prove more expensive, it would last longer. However, Coode's plan prevailed, and the iron bridge which was opened in 1895 survived until 1984, despite the steadily increasing traffic flows. A new, stone-fronted bridge was then erected (not without controversy) on dry land further on the Portland side, and the seawater successfully diverted through it.

If the building of the Ferry Bridge began to break Portland's isolation; the railways did the rest. For a promontory of vertiginous steeps and deeps, the island had a remarkable number of railway lines. The first railway in Dorset was the horse-drawn Merchant's Railway which opened in 1826, for the transportation of stone from Tophill to the harbour at Castletown. The first passenger line to be built was between Weymouth and Chiswell in 1863.This sloshed its way over Weymouth Marsh, proceeding via Rodwell, and crossing Small Mouth on a twenty-seven span wooden viaduct, which looked as rickety and unreliable as some clapped-out fairground ride. (It was replaced by a slightly re-aligned steel bridge in 1902.) The line travelled parallel to Chesil Bank on the harbour side of the causeway, where sections of the bed are still visible, and on to a station in Victoria Square, Chiswell (formerly the site of a poorhouse). Hardy's hero Pierston travelled along the line in *The Well-Beloved*.

> Since the days of his youth a railway had been constructed along the pebble bank, so that, except when the rails were washed away by the tides, which was rather often, the peninsula was quickly accessible. At two o' clock in the afternoon he was rattled along by this new means

> of locomotion, under the familiar monotonous line of bran-coloured stones, and he soon emerged from the station, which stood as a strange exotic among the black lerrets, the ruins of the washed-away village, and the white cubes of oolite, just come to view after burial through unreckonable geological years.

Delays in construction meant that the opening of this invader went unannounced, as had happened before with the Weymouth-Bristol line. Various extensions were proposed; some were never built. The line was closed to passengers in 1952, but the damage had already been done. 'Island' was now a courtesy title for Portland.

*

At the Ferry Bridge end of the causeway two ill-assorted buildings faced each other across the road. On the harbour side was the extensive Whitehead Torpedo Works, and on the Fleet side, among the fields, was the Weymouth Port Authority Sanitary Hospital. The Works site is now covered with housing, but part of the H-shaped Hospital building is still visible, though crowded about with the caravans of the Chesil Vista holiday park.

The Hospital was erected in 1880, its architect was George Rackstraw Crickmay, Weymouth neighbour of the Falkner family, and one-time employer of Thomas Hardy. It was purpose-built, on land which had previously belonged to the Ferry Bridge Commissioners, and great attention was paid to detail. Crickmay's architectural drawings and specifications still exist. The plans show a pleasant and spacious set

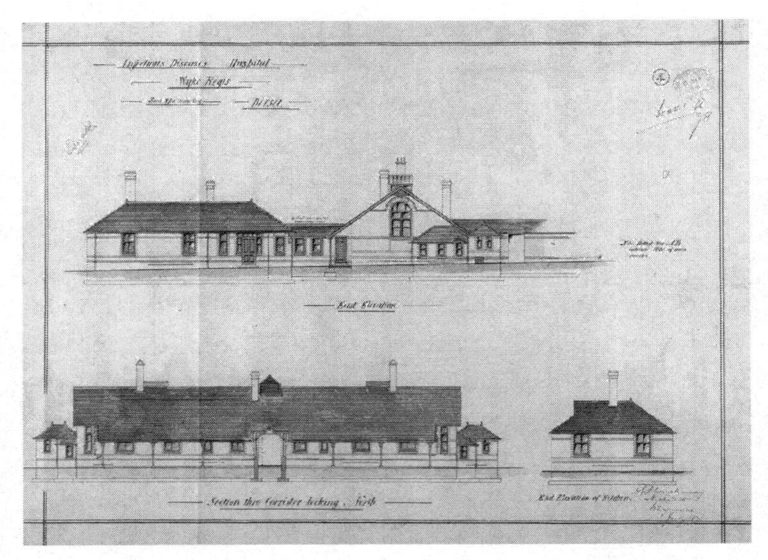

Plan for 'Infectious Diseases Hospital, Wyke Regis' by G R Crickmay, 1879.

of buildings, while another, anonymous, document headed 'Furnishing and General Administration of a Small Isolation Hospital' offers eleven cyclostyled pages of suggestions for best practice. Iron bedsteads are recommended, with horse-hair mattresses and bedside lockers, as 'patients like to have a few things near them'. Easy chairs should have removable cushions. The value of portable food containers for keeping food hot in transit is discussed, along with the best choice of bath. Regarding the staff, it is recommended that the hospital porter should preferably live nearby and be readily available, as the removal of corpses was best done under cover of night.

Isolation hospitals were fashionable in that period – towns such as Bridport and Sturminster Newton possessed them – but the Weymouth hospital was specifically built to serve the port. A massive ledger, the Inspectors' Journal, provides a record of the inspection of all the ships which entered the Harbour from 1911–1968. The Inspectors had the authority to issue notices about such issues as insanitary WCs, vermin infestations, defective chimneys and the like. There was no floating hospital in the Harbour, and so (despite protests to the Admiralty) those with cholera, yellow fever and even bubonic plague were landed at Castletown Pier and transported by ambulance to Ferry Bridge. Patients with venereal diseases were treated there too, and – although there were other isolation hospitals in Weymouth, at Radipole Lane and on Coldharbour Hill – various local cases were taken to Ferry Bridge.

This was not ideal. In May 1909, for example, there was an outbreak of scarlet fever in the Tophill district of Portland, and Easton School was closed. While most of the sufferers were isolated in their own houses, seven cases were removed to the Hospital. There must have been a great risk of cross-infection.

The building was designed for forty patients and soon became too small. A report in 1912 by Weymouth's Medical Officer of Health, Dr Howard, stated that the Hospital was under-staffed. As a result, patients had to empty their own bedpans and slops, and perform menial work. The ordering system was said to be inefficient. And it was remarked that, should they receive a typhoid patient, the staff would be unable to cope, because they could not provide any individual attention.

The remaining papers on the Hospital sometimes give

the impression of near-chaos. There were rumours that the oysters in the Fleet were being poisoned by its waste, and a more serious charge came after an outbreak of smallpox in 1911, when 'three or four cases' were taken to the Hospital on the 12th of April. (On April 13th a further victim was transferred from the SS *Iran*.) The Sanitary Inspector complained that contaminated bedding had been thrown into the harbour, and 'a mattress was washed up on the foreshore near the Torpedo Works'. Two children had picked up bedding and carried it into Wyke village. In his reply, Dr Howard assured the Inspector that 'definite action should be taken'.

In 1914 the Clerk, J J Roberts notified Howard that the body of a deceased patient, Captain Alexander McKegg, had been buried in the hospital grounds during the smallpox epidemic, 'with Canon Davies officiating'. McKegg's family requested a memorial, and Roberts wrote again to confirm that there was 'nothing in the Burial Act to prevent a headstone being erected'. The Chairman objected, not unreasonably remarking that he did not want the surrounding land 'to look like a burial ground'. He suggested that a headstone be erected in Wyke churchyard instead.

There were other small tragedies. A newly-released patient was found wandering helplessly about, and was taken by a passerby to Weymouth, while in 1925 the Clerk to the Borough Magistrates wrote to Dr Howard about an incident when a man was found drowned in the Fleet. He was carried to the Hospital mortuary, but was refused admittance and had to be unceremoniously placed in the shed of a public house which, wrote the Clerk, 'is not a very seemly place to leave a body'.

The Hospital closed in the 1930s and in April 1937 an auction of the two acre site was held on the premises. The structure was said to be in sound condition, and credit was given to the contractor, who had also been responsible for building the London Law Courts. In all, four smallpox victims had been buried in the grounds, but potential buyers were reassured that their bodies had since been exhumed and reburied in Weymouth. The hospital was sold at the auction to a man named Batchelor for the sum of £2,000. The site was by now a desirable one as there was, as the auctioneer noted, 'quiet development of land adjoining'. The building became a technical school, but since the 1950s has been part of a holiday camp, with some of the original buildings in its midst.

Isolation in Portland has come to a double end.

Lagoon

The lake is good for nothing except sea-fowl,
herons, and oysters...

John Meade Falkner, *Moonfleet*

Below the clustering caravans of the Chesil Vista holiday park in Wyke Regis there is an oyster farm. Oysters here are nothing new, though the village of Wyke itself has changed enormously over the years. According to Hutchins, the word means 'a curving or reach of the sea, or winding of the sea.' Driving through the village, along the crowded road to the causeway, gives no sense of the sea at all. Modern Wyke has no conspicuous boundaries either, though an ancient charter helpfully lists those which were there in 988, when the parish was much larger, reaching far into what is now modern Weymouth.

From the West Sea to Saggeloth
From Saggeloth to Muleditch,
From Muleditch to Blackstone,
From Blackstone to Goldcroft,
From Goldcroft to Soreditch,
From Soreditch to Lodmore,
And from Lodmore to the East Sea.

Oysters usually thrive in the lagoon at Wyke, as it is sheltered by Chesil Bank, here almost at its highest, close to the Isle of Portland. These oysters are cultivated; at other sites along the Fleet naturally-occurring oysters can be found.

The banks below the villages of Langton Herring and Rodden are composed of Fuller's Earth in which oyster beds have for centuries flourished in 'a thick accumulation'. Fleet oysters were mentioned in the thirteenth century, but they have actually grown here since Roman times; their fossilised remains are in evidence among the flotsam on the lagoon's shore. In an agreement of 1427, Abbotsbury monastery paid the fishermen a paltry 2d for every 200 oysters they supplied – while even a single salmon was worth as much as 6d.

Farmed oysters arrived later. In 1743, there was an attempt to establish oyster beds in the Fleet at Wyke. The seed oysters were brought in from 'Conkall near Saint Malo' and were judged to be a 'very poor sort of oyster', though much improved by their being 'properly managed on the English Oister Grounds'. When grown at Colchester the shells of these European Flat oysters acquired green tips, but unfortunately the oysters did not take kindly to the conditions in the Fleet, and failed to thrive.

In 1792, two hundred of the oysters were harvested, only to be stolen and sold in Weymouth by a man named as Thomas Orr. (How he contrived to do this is not mentioned.) By the time of Orr's theft, the second Earl of Ilchester was lord of the manor, and while he could do little about the oysters' disappearance, he tightened up on other, more lucrative, poaching practices. In 1800 he appointed a gamekeeper to:

> Seize and take all and all manner of Guns, Bows, Dogs,Teirels, [Falcons?], Trammils [Hawks?], Lowbals, Hays or other Nets, Hare Pipes, Wires, Snares or other Instruments for taking Swans, Rabbits, Hares, Pheasants, Partridges and Game of any kind, and all manner of Fishing Nets, Angles [small fishing hooks], Leaps, Pipes, Baskets, Lines, Hooks or other Instruments or Engines for taking Fish, etc.

This draconian list was included in an essay on Abbotsbury in the Dorset Natural History and Antiquarian Field Club's *Proceedings* for 1927. Responding from Holland House in London, the sixth Earl of Ilchester commented mildly:

> As you twice refer to the oyster beds at Wyke being no longer in existence, it may interest you to know the reason. My father found the sale of oysters to the public was not paying as we could seldom dredge in bulk, but continued to use the beds for our own private consumption, relaying oysters of fair size every two or three years. This continued until the war. At the end of it, I had the beds dredged, and found nothing alive on them.
>
> At the time we blamed slop drains from a neighbouring camp, but I am nowadays inclined to think that the serious epidemics which had everywhere so depleted our British oysters, may have caught us early and have been the cause.

Ilchester concluded by stating that, oysters being so expensive, he would be unlikely to try farming them again – though he hinted, 'I might let the beds, should I get an offer to take them'.

Oysters had become a luxury food, as epidemics and over-fishing seriously limited their production. In the eighteenth and nineteenth centuries, they had been a popular street food for poor people. Woodbury Hill, above Bere Regis in Dorset, was the site of one of the largest and most popular of fairs, where hundreds of oysters were consumed. The fair has long gone, but oyster shells still litter the unpopulated grassy slopes.

In 1990 oyster farming returned to the Fleet. The Hon. Charlotte Townshend, the latest of the Strangways to inherit the estate, went into partnership with Neville Copperthwaite, and Abbotsbury Oyster Farm began. They chose to grow Pacific oysters, because they are fast-growing and more immune to disease than the native ones. The French Bag and Trestle method was used (that is, net bags laid on trestles in the water) with juvenile oysters brought from a hatchery. These took three years to reach market size.

In 2004 the declining farm was taken over by another company, who decided to employ a innovatory Australian method of oyster farming, using timber posts and rails carrying plastic mesh baskets. Part-grown oysters are imported from the Channel Islands and placed in the Fleet for up to a year. All this, they say, is easily accomplished by one man and his dog!

The Crab House Café, on the Wyke shore of the Fleet, has the oysters on its menu. In good weather, they can be eaten at outdoor tables, under fluttering umbrellas of flamingo-pink, close to the beds which supplied them.

Beside the café and oyster beds is the landing-place for the Fleet Observer. This small craft has a flat glass bottom, enabling passengers (on a fine day) to see what is happening beneath, as well as around them. The boat lies low in the inky-black, silent and salty waters of the East Fleet, between the clay cliffs and the Chesil Bank. Though the lagoon is shallow, it is bedded in sticky clinging mud, and there are hidden sandbanks along this stretch. The bed of the Fleet still belongs to the Strangways family, while Chesil Bank itself belongs to the Crown between Portland and Wyke.

Rowing boats are stacked on the shores of nearby Pirates Cove, and opposite them on the Chesil stand a number of traditional beach huts, some of them stained a sinister pitch-black. Though such huts are an expensive commodity along the Dorset coast, these sparse wooden dwellings are strictly for the Adela Curtises of the twenty-first century. Everything which might be needed has to be rowed across from the landward side, there is no mains electricity or water, and sewage has to be physically removed by the owner.

Along the Bank, fences are erected to keep foxes from the nesting site of the rare little terns, which make a brief visit each year before flying back to South Africa. This is their most southerly site in England. A twenty-four hour watch is kept during the nesting season, to protect them from another of their main predators: human beings.

Hares also frequent the beach, and oyster-catchers and cormorants can be glimpsed among the thieving gulls. The surface of the beach is scarred and pitted with *cans*, produced when the sea surges through the pebbles into the Fleet, causing the shingle to collapse into hollows.

The boat turns back just before the Narrows, where the tides are tricky. Wyke Regis church is high above, a reassuring landmark for ships in the bay. Due south of the church, at the base of the grimy clay cliffs of Pirates Cove, are the remains of a Neolithic salt mine. This was accidentally discovered in 1960 by Mrs S Palmer of London SW6, 'together with her daughter'. They had been exploring the shore, picking up pebbles, when they noticed a quantity of potsherds, some of which they took to the Museum in Dorchester. Three of the Museum's members explored the site 'between the tides' and found a hearth and two types of pottery – small beakers and larger, coarser, vessels, all with flat rims – from which they conjectured that salt was boiled on the hearth in the larger vessels and the flakes collected in the smaller ones, in an early example of the exploitation of the Fleet.

The road beside Wyke church leads down between bungalows, and some discreetly-sited caravans, across the sea meadows to the Bridging Hard. The Army first made their mark here in the First World War, when the area behind the Hard was occupied by their huts. In 1928 a contingent of the Royal Engineers spent a month camping above the Fleet, where they were trained in bridge-building across the Narrows (displacing local fishermen in the process). From their primitive camp the soldiers – the first of many – emerged to build pontoon bridges. Cavalry riders swam across the rapid waters with their horses alongside them. By the 1970s about 30,000 soldiers were training there every year.

> The facilities and training were considered second to none, covering basic combat training, range firing,

> infantry tactics, map reading, field defences, mine laying, demolition work, water supply, watermanship, rafting, armoured personnel carrier flotation, canoeing and orienteering – but bridging still took pride of place, for Wyke Regis was acknowledged as the best place in Britain for such training.
>
> Doug Hollings, *A History of Wyke Regis*

The camp is still in use: an assortment of buildings, topped by scrawls of barbed wire. The effect is ugly: aesthetics evidently have no part in the training of soldiers. Beyond the camp, the lagoon opens out into Littlesea, its widest section, where the sudden influx of water disperses the tides, and they become progressively weaker for the rest of their course. The tides rise in the Fleet when the sea in the Channel is falling. Simultaneously, it can be high tide in the Fleet and low tide out in the sea.

The most ambitious of all the enterprises which have been tried along this section of the Fleet was the attempt in the 1630s – in a period of reclamation – to drain the land for use as pasture by a group of 'gentlemen adventurers', led by Sir George Horsey. Peter Mundy, a traveller through this part of Dorset in 1635, dismissed their attempt to change the nature of the 'indraught': 'whereon was spent great sommes of money in makeinge of sluces, trenches, etts. [and other] Inventions to keepe the Tide from comeing in, as also to let out what is within. But as yet all is to little purpose, the maine sea soakeing through the beach all alonge.'

A modern commentator, Christopher Taylor, likewise regarded the scheme as 'far-fetched and ill-considered'.

Despite controls, seawater continued to pour over the Bank and leach through the pebbles. The lagoon is also fed on the landward side by little crystalline streams flowing down the valleys from the hills above the Fleet – one stream makes its way round Chapel Hill in Abbotsbury, two come from Portesham, one of which enters the Fleet at the Swannery, while another comes from Langton Herring. Together, they turn the waters of the West Fleet brackish, diluting the salt, while adding to the volume of water.

In a comprehensive account of the draining of the Fleet, Gordon Le Pard describes how in 1630 the adventurers planned at 'their own proper costs to drayne a certayne Meere Fleete or parcel of Saltmarsh' belonging to Sir John Strangways. In return for his permission, Strangways would receive the whole of the West Fleet, which formed the Abbotsbury section of the lagoon. The West Fleet was 'severed' from the East by 'an ancient banke, ridge or causeway called Bridgehill'. The causeway survives, south-east of Shipmoor Point, and close to the Swannery. It is a stone road, made of Forest Marble, with shingle filling the gaps between the stones. Carts were able to cross the Fleet here; in a manoeuvre far simpler than crossing the lagoon by trow, and then exchanging the boats for lerrets on the beach. The lerrets enabled them to fish in the open sea, and they afterwards returned in the same way with their day's catch. Believed to be of late medieval (and therefore monastic) origin, the causeway is visible – though not accessible – today.

Work had not long begun before the Strangways' ownership of the Fleet was challenged – and not for the first time. It was claimed by George Kercke, a Groom of the King's

Bedchamber, that, as the Fleet was salty (or at least brackish), it was an arm of the sea, and therefore belonged to the Crown. If this was the case, Strangways' rights would have been confined to the keeping of swans, fishing and reed-cutting. Kercke's claim was initially successful, but he seems to have been misled as to how much work needed to be done, and soon abandoned the scheme.

A second attempt at drainage by Kercke in 1633 was no more effective than its predecessor had been. Apparently assuming that the Chesil would act as a watertight barrier, a dam was built between it and the land, and equipped with sluice-gates which proved unable to withstand the pressure of water. Traces of the sluices and other controls have never been found, but they were obviously most likely to have been erected in the Narrows. The theory was that if they were exposed and washed free of salt by the rain, the mudflats between Fleet and Wyke would have provided a rich ground for pasture.

It seems odd that they have left no signs of their presence. In his article 'The Lost Wall', C F Bird remarked that 'Possible alignments for this structure can be seen on air photographs, but on investigation these have proved to be dredged boat channels, outfall pipes, cable lines, and minor shore constructions such as groynes and boat launching-ramps.'

Evidence, but little information, remains about another scheme, known as 'Fry's Works', or 'the Frying Pan'. In 1665 William Fry was granted a ninety-nine year lease by John Strangways to dam the lagoon at Herbury by building an embayment wall enclosing a ten acre section of water. Herbury is a peninsula jutting out into the water by Moonfleet Manor, which is also known as 'Donkey Island' (it is sometimes an island at high tide). Once an area of rough grass, where the Weymouth donkeys over-wintered (they must have trotted there all the way from the sands), Herbury is now arable. In this section of the Fleet, Chesil Bank is greening over, as it is difficult to reach on foot. Access is only permitted in winter months and the wild life flourishes: mullet leap in the lagoon, samphire grows low on the peninsula, and ravens lurk unkindly on the shore.

There are still hollows in the earth around Fry's Works, marking the areas from which the stone was quarried for building the embayment wall. The footings of the wall sometimes emerge at low tide, making it possible to walk across the water at this point on an accidental causeway.

In 1935, there was a plan to build an aircraft bombing station on the Fleet, to the east of Abbotsbury, as part of the preparations for war. The plan was bitterly contested by the fishermen who would lose their livelihoods, and by ornithologists and by conservationists – who, surprisingly enough, were successful in their campaign.

A far greater threat to Herbury came in the 1980s, when the Central Electricity Generating Board put forward a proposal to build an enormous nuclear power station in Herbury Cove – a sly move, as it did not mention its precise position on the Fleet. Few people had heard of Herbury; mention of the Fleet or of Chesil Bank would have provoked immediate and furious opposition. This tactic was noted by the House of Commons Select Committee when they examined the scheme (which they opposed). In the end, Hinckley Point was chosen for the site of the new power station.

The lagoon below neighbouring Langton Herring, darkened by reeds, is eerie, silent and languorous. The village is safely inland, with its back set firmly against the water. The coastal path, too, soon turns inland, avoiding the Abbotsbury Swannery where the Fleet again widens, no longer tidal, to dwindle and shrink to nothing in a scrubby ditch below the stronghold of the Subtropical Gardens. The lagoon may once have stretched further (to the south as well as to the west); there are occasional patches of water towards Burton Bradstock. As a visitors' leaflet explains, further evidence of the Fleet's previous extent is provided every winter, 'when storms excavate large peat blocks, the floor of the ancient lagoon, from beneath the seaward side of the beach'. It is suggested that the Fleet was formed at around the same time as Chesil Bank. Driven by rising sea levels after the last Ice Age, huge quantities of rock debris rolled inland. In forming the Bank, they trapped the lagoon against the land.

Like the lagoon, the Bank too may once have gone further. When he was sitting on the shingle at Fleet in 1897, addressing the members of the Dorset Field Club, Vaughan Cornish argued that it could have extended from 'Eype mouth, a little west of Bridport, to Chesilton', with a break across West Bay.

While writing his novel *On Chesil Beach*, Ian McEwan innocently picked up pebbles from different stretches of the beach to test the famous theory of the pebbles' grading. Taking the samples home, McEwan put them on his mantelpiece. When this was discovered there was quite a furore (although many a West Dorset garden must be harbouring its own selection of the stones). Eventually, some friends returned the pebbles for him, replacing each stone in its rightful section of the Bank. Ninety years previously, to illustrate the article which formed the basis of his talk, Cornish too had collected 'samples to show grading' and photographed them. No one then found this activity worth remarking.

This is a fragile landscape, and has been much exploited. (There was even an unrealised plan to prospect for gold in the Fleet waters.) Should any of the drainage schemes have succeeded, the Swannery would have been lost. For years it was the most valuable resource along the Fleet, and it continues to be the centrepiece – the feathered crown – of the entire length of Chesil Beach.

A Lamentation of Swans

The woods decay, the woods decay and fall,
The vapours weep their burthen to the ground,
Man comes and tills the soil and lies beneath,
And after many a summer dies the swan.

Alfred Tennyson, '*Tithonus*'

When the mute swan dies – so the legend says – it gives voice to a haunting, elegiac song, breaking the silence of a lifetime. This belief, which reaches back to classical times, continues to have a wistful appeal. In 1886 the composer Camille Saint-Saëns responded to the legend with a melancholic piece called 'Le Cygne' (The Swan) which formed the thirteenth of the fourteen movements of his *Carnival of the Animals*. 'Le Cygne' was the only section of the work which he allowed to be performed in public while he was still alive. Mindful of his posthumous reputation, he regarded the other movements, with their cuckoos and kangaroos, as too light-hearted for serious consideration. The work was intended, after all, as a musical joke.

'Le Cygne' was used as the music for a ballet of the same name, which was choreographed by the dancer Michel Fokine. As a child, Fokine trained at the Imperial Ballet School in St Petersburg. A talented dancer, he was well-versed too in both Russian and foreign literature, and Tennyson's early poem 'The Dying Swan' provided him with the subject of his ballet. In the poem the bird is floating down a lonely river, among the marshes and the withy-beds. As he is carried along the water 'The desolate creeks and pools among,/Were flooded over with eddying song.' The swan is lamenting his imminent death.

In 1905, Fokine's near-contemporary at the ballet school, Anna Pavlova, asked him to create a dance for her. He had been Pavlova's first partner; they had appeared together in 'Arlequinade' at the Mariinsky Theatre, which was attached to the Imperial Ballet School. Fokine reflected on the long and graceful neck and softly fluid movements of the ballerina, and 'Le Cygne' was the result: a dance which will be forever associated with Anna Pavlova, who performed it more than four thousand times. In 1931, the year of Pavlova's death, Fokine told *Dance Magazine* 'The dance became the symbol of the New Russian Ballet. It was a combination of masterful technique with expressiveness. It was like a proof that the dance could and should satisfy not only the eye, but through the medium of the eye should penetrate the soul.'

Pavlova wrote that she had been fascinated by swans ever since she had seen them as a child in a St Petersburg park. When on the water, they are elegant creatures, whose movements and displays, combined with their cries, are expressive of many moods. (Mute swans are not truly mute; merely quieter than Bewick's, or any other of the seven species of swans.) Sleeked feathers suggest uncertainty, for instance, and raised feathers ('making a hood') mean aggression. Swans naturally adopt beautiful poses when preening and sleeping – when afloat, they are natural ballerinas.

Anna Pavlova made her home in England in 1912, at the balconied Ivy House on Hampstead Heath. The garden lawns swept down a small lake, on which she kept her two pet swans (she had something of a menagerie at the house). Photographs show her gracefully entwined together with Jack, her favourite swan, on the grass. 'I watch the swans,' she wrote, 'then I call Fifi, the gazelle, and then I don't take myself so seriously. Why? Because I realise that nature is greater than art.'

Nature and art came memorably together in the late 1920s, when Pavlova visited Abbotsbury Swannery with her corps de ballet, who were rehearsing for a production of the second act of Tchaikovsky's ballet *Swan Lake* – which ends with its own, immortal, dance of a dying swan. The dancers probably travelled there by train on the Abbotsbury branch line from the junction at Upwey, though little is known about this unusual visit. Three tiny photographs remain as proof of the happening, snapped by the Revd Edward Victor Tanner.

Tanner, who taught at Weymouth College, was a tireless and invaluable recorder of the unexpected, the lowly and the not-altogether-respectable. From 1922 he was a major contributor to the Dorset Photographic Survey. His pictures here show a set of disdainful swans, apparently unimpressed

*Pavlova's corp de ballet dancing with the swans (*E V Tanner*)*

by the vigorously twirling tutus of the dancers on the shore of the Fleet. Fred Lexster, who later became the swanherd, stands sturdily in the midst of them, gamely playing his role in this open-air performance. In a second photograph, Pavlova herself looks on. Wrapped in a fur-trimmed suit, she is a remote and deceptively fragile figure, absorbed by the sight of so many swans.

The birds, accustomed to visitors and contented with their lot, appear – as Harvey Darton observed in his *Marches of Wessex*, 1922 – 'very highly civilised'. But swans can be dangerous: they must always be treated with respect, as Darton discovered for himself when he visited the Swannery.

> The veteran keeper once…pulled an old cob off his nest for me (the male and female take turns on the eggs), to show his weapons of offence. The keeper wore thick leather gaiters. The angry bird hissed, and put all his hackles up: his neck became like a nutmeg-grater meant for cocoanuts. He pecked: and the sound on the gaiters was as that of a hammer. Then he spread his huge wings, and slapped with the outer pinions. It was as if a cane was being beaten on wood. And then he drew himself more erect. But at that the keeper for a moment deftly caught a wing pinion and pulled the wing out for me to see, the bird, still half tame, half wild, merely swearing. The keeper showed me the last weapon: a terrific knob, with a queer little hook in it, at the elbow joint [which] had broken three ribs of an under-keeper not long ago.

The swans are free to come and go as they please, but usually choose to stay, as the Fleet waters provide them with their omnivorous diet. Come the winter, though, many of them make off eastwards towards the saltier waters near the Causeway, where their favourite eel grass is more plentiful, returning to the Swannery in the spring. The eel grass is essential to their diet. In the harsh winter of 1880, for example, the Fleet froze to the depth of about a foot. The eel grass clung to the bottom of the ice and was removed by the tides. As a result, many swans died of starvation.

In high summer the swans are grounded for several weeks while they moult, becoming as flightless as ostriches. Their discarded feathers are not wasted: the primary feathers are sent to Lloyds of London where, converted into quill pens, they are used by the underwriters for inscribing shipping accidents in their Doom Book. Other, shorter feathers are gathered up daily and sent to the Plumery in Chiswick, which claims to be 'the only manufacturer of horse hair, feather, and wool military plumage in the world'. Here they are sewn into the plumes which crest the helmets of the Queen's Gentlemen-at-Arms.

Swan feathers are also used for artists' brushes and arrow flights – and, more particularly, to make the brushes used by bee-keepers for removing bees from the honeycomb. Thus honoured, but temporarily marooned, the swans sit out the moulting season until once again they can launch into flight. Harvey Darton provides an awed description of this moment.

> It is a wonderful sight, that great lagoon covered by vast snowflakes: wonderful to behold the heavy uprising of a flight of them, from the water, scuttering along like an aeroplane before it lifts, for their bodies are heavy: wonderful also to see the tremendous impetus with which they touch the water again and rush through it till the resistance stops them: most wonderful of all to hear the glorious metallic clang of their wings as eight or ten in a V-shaped formation fly over your head, their beautiful long necks straight, their noble pinions flapping strongly in the tremendous carriage of their body.

As they swim, the swans are accompanied by a flotilla of lesser birds: such as coots, mallards and those tiresome invaders, Canada geese. Their escort may also include a few rarer additions – a pair of black swans for instance, or for some years an American flamingo (nicknamed Rosy), presumably an escapee from a private collection, who proudly stalked the shore in her frivolous pink feathers. As the writer John Fowles commented on sighting the bird, 'a wild South American flamingo in an English sheep-meadow belongs much more to Lewis Carroll than ornithology'.

The swans, though, are a familiar sight here. The 'game of swannes' have remained at Abbotsbury for centuries. The first mention of the Swannery and swanherd William Squilor was in the Court Roll of 1395. They were then the property of the monks, whose ruined abbey overhangs the village. The Benedictine monastery was founded in the eleventh century, shortly before the Norman Conquest, and the swans were kept not for their ornamental qualities but as a source of food. Only the cygnets are edible: full-grown birds taste of the mud and silt in which they forage.

After the Dissolution of the Monasteries in 1539, the Abbotsbury estate was bought by Sir Giles Strangways; and has remained ever since in the same family, who later became the earls of Ilchester. The swans, too, have stayed in the possession of the Ilchester estate. For identification they are ringed and nicked on the outside of the web. This mark is called the 'hive of Abbotsbury'. (*Hive* or *hythe* was the dialect word for an inlet. The poet William Barnes in his entry on 'hythe' in his Dorset dialect glossary of 1886 remarks that 'the old Saxon word is yet living among us by Portland, for the hythes at which the fish are landed on the coast that borders on the Fleet, as Chickerell hythe, Langton hythe &tc.')

Such an ownership is very uncommon. Most of the mute swans in England can be claimed by the Queen (should she so wish), though on the Thames some of the swans traditionally belong to the Worshipful Companies of Vintners and Dyers. Every July the companies hold a swan-upping from Sunbury to Abingdon, when the swans are counted, checked and marked. If a painting by Stanley Spencer of a frantic, flapping swan-upping at Cookham can be relied on, this was once a very frenzied event, with the birds soaring off in every direction.

Not only do the Ilchester family own 'the flight of swans', they also own most of the Fleet lagoon, and not just the floor of it, as a nineteenth-century document made clear.

> Lord Ilchester is Lord of the Manors of the two extreme parishes on the Fleet Water, Abbotsbury and Wyke, and of all the charters and confirmations both before and since the dissolution of the monasteries, owner of the waters of the Fleet along the shores of the intermediate parishes, and of the soil thereof from end to end.

Verification of the complexities of the ownership of the Fleet was expensively obtained by three fishermen from Fleet parish in 1806, after they had 'discreetly and unjustly' fished in the lagoon, which was 'the property of, the Right Honourable the Earl of Ilchester'. They were spotted by one of the earl's tenants who 'justly caused a prosecution to be commenced'. By way of reparation, they were obliged to apologise in the *Western Flying Post* on June 23rd, 1806. Two weeks later they were forced to advertise once again in the newspaper. They were, they explained, 'poor and ignorant men, scarcely able to read, write, or understand' and were now acknowledging their mistake in not realising that other parts of the Fleet in other parishes, belong to 'the Lords of the Manors whose lands they adjoin'.

There were many similar cases. Ownership of land and water – even of the fish out in the sea – seems to have been vigorously enforced, right from monastic times. In 1269, it was stated that the Abbot had the first pick of any catch, and 'as much of it as he pleases'. And in 1315 came a declaration that 'wreck, Great Fish and whatever else is thrown up by the sea upon the land of the Abbot belongs to him'.

The restrictions continued unchanged after the Strangways acquired the estate. In 1791, for instance, anyone using 'Boats or troughs [trows] in the part of water known as the Fleet' was liable to prosecution and the destruction of his boat. A letter of 1797 asserted that the Earl of Ilchester had the right to claim everything that was taken up above the high water mark.

Nor were the Abbotsbury villagers allowed to shoot wild fowl. In 1810 a letter from the Sergeant's Inn listed all the forbidden birds, which included mallards, duck, teal and widgeon – though not the humble coot, presumably because its meat, like that of the swans, was not worth eating. The penalty for illicit shooting was three months in gaol.

Other activities were regulated, too. In 1850 William Jennings, solicitor, produced a draft bill warning that 'if donkeys, horses or other cattle' were found grazing anywhere on the manor 'the same would be impounded'.

Unless employed by the estate, it must have been difficult for anyone to earn a living in such circumstances.

When it came to swan-killing, suspects were pursued even further afield. In winter, some of the Abbotsbury swans travelled as far as Weymouth, to Lodmore or the Backwater. Occasionally they were shot by unwitting holiday-makers (among them in 1865 a twelve-year-old boy). In 1867, another boy and a 'pensioner' aged fifty-seven were charged with shooting one of the swans in Weymouth Bay in a case reported in the *Weymouth & Portland Guardian* of April 20th. The pair pleaded ignorance of the law. 'Appearing for the noble lord', Mr Baskett of Evershot said that the swan was 'a peculiar sort of bird': it was a 'species of valuable property, such as a horse or sheep'. The swan was a Royal Bird, 'kept by Lord Ilchester at great expense, not for his own pleasure, but for the public benefit'. The swan, Mr. Baskett concluded, was 'an ornament to Weymouth Bay'.

When Sir Giles Strangways bought the Swannery after the Dissolution of the Monasteries, he also acquired the manor, the surrounding lands, and St Peter's Abbey, building himself a house with stone from the ruins. Under fierce siege from the Parliamentarians in the Civil War, his castle was burnt to the ground in 1644.

In 1765 Elizabeth, first Countess of Ilchester (heroine of one of Hardy's stories in *A Group of Noble Dames*) built another castle in Strawberry Hill Gothic style on an outcrop above the Abbotsbury shore and close to the beach road, as a summer home for the Strangways family. Only the great sandstone outer walls on the southern side of the site now remain, as the original castle was destroyed by a fire in the

Hyacinth Room during a blizzard of 1913. (The house-keeper and maid had lit fires to welcome the family's arrival with disastrous consequences.) A replacement castle was erected shortly afterwards in 1915, but this massive building proved to be faulty and damp and was scarcely ever used. It was summarily demolished in 1934.

Detached from the house, in a sheltered hollow between the castle and the sea, Elizabeth planted what was intended as a kitchen garden. Surprisingly, in such a treeless setting, the garden flourished:

> The hills provide shelter from the coldest winds, an early planting of tamarisk and evergreen oaks breaks the strength of the salt-laden south-westerlies blowing in off the sea, while the chances of frost are reduced by the warmth of the deep water off the Chesil Bank, which shelves rapidly. Equally importantly, the heart of the garden lies over Abbotsbury's only area of sandy soil, providing an opportunity to create a garden of unusual interest.
>
> John Fair & Don Moxom, *Abbotsbury & the Swannery*

Along Chesil Beach there are other such stretches, with their own maritime micro-climate, such as the gardens of Moonfleet Manor and the Manor in West Bexington. According to Thomas Hardy, Portland itself stretches 'so far into mid-sea that touches of the Gulf Stream soften the air till February'.

Elizabeth's work was just the beginning. Later members of the family added to and extended the garden, planting a protective wood, and bringing plants from far-flung countries. The gardens used to contain peacocks, whose unexpected shrieking echoed through the trees. Now every October, brilliant fairground colours illuminate the Subtropical Gardens as dusk turns to dark, bringing out the startling freakishness of some of the plants, and throwing other hidden growths into sudden prominence. Multi-coloured theatrical lighting is used, creating huge architectural shapes and shadows, while candles line the pathways.

Older than Strangways Castle and its garden, older than the Abbey, is yet another ruin, one which surmounts the village. Abbotsbury Castle is an Iron Age hill fort at the beginning of the Dorset Ridgeway, a great mound cresting the steep coastal road leading to the west. The fort is triangular in shape, its massive earth ramparts still present on the landward sides. The site was excavated in 1974, (amongst the finds were sling stones) though the interior was left undisturbed, because, as the archaeologist noted, it was 'superbly preserved'.

On the road is a lay-by, used as a viewing point for one of the most celebrated of Dorset scenes. St Catherine's Chapel, the Chesil and the Swannery stretch out below. Here too, the Fleet widens expansively before its disappearance below the Subtropical Gardens. The track along the hill fort's summit provides even vaster views. On rare clear days, you can see the entire stretch of Lyme Bay, from Portland Bill to Start Point in Devon, surrounded by an immensity of sea. Turn inland, and there are long reaches of hills and settled fields below, with scarcely a building in sight.

*

Follies are thin on the ground in dignified Dorset. One example, a landmark which can be seen from the coast, is Hardy's Monument on Black Down. The monument is a cumbersome tower, shaped like an upturned spy-glass, and named after Thomas Hardy – Nelson's sea captain, that is, and not the writer, which makes it a disappointment to many visitors. Chesil Bank does have a folly of its own, though it is one that now passes almost unnoticed, being nudged by bungalows and recently divided into three dwellings. Like all of the main roads out of Weymouth, the one through Wyke is blighted by ribbon development, creeping up towards the coast. Wyke Castle is on the crest of the built-up Westhill Road, on a difficult corner site close to the village's old coastguard cottages. It adjoins a track rather speculatively called Pirates Lane, a slippery slope running down to the lagoon and Pirates Cove. Though the name 'Pirate' may sound rather bogus, it does in fact have some age. (It was formerly called Green Lane.) During the descent the landscape suddenly shifts to one of squattered fields of caravans and sheds, with piebald ponies grazing the rough grass.

What the castle does still have is a grandstand view of sea and sky, lagoon and beach. In 1851 Dr Andrew Chadwick Fenoulhet acquired 'All that Close or Meadow or pasture called Colloways Close or Bohays containing by estimation 1.5 acres at Wyke Regis' for the sum of £230. On this land he built his piece of Victorian 'nonsense' for himself and his large family, a frivolity which took a more serious face when it became Wyke's first medical practice.

The building, of squared Portland stone, is V-shaped, and is based on the design of the Martello towers which keep a watchful eye along the coast. It has a round central tower, with a second square tower at the end of each arm. The round tower has a glass roof, and the building has 360 degree panoramic views. As befits a castle, there is even a dungeon, containing a fresh-water well.

In the early 1920s Wyke Castle was bought by the ornithologist Edmund Selous and his wife Fanny Margaret Maxwell. Born in 1863, Fanny was the third of six children of Mary Elizabeth Braddon, prolific author of works which included the sensational novel *Lady Audley's Secret*. Mrs Braddon gave birth to all of her six children before she was able to marry their father. In 1923, while living at the castle, Fanny founded Weymouth Women's Institute, becoming its first president.

Edmund Selous (1857–1934) practised briefly as a barrister before devoting the rest of his life to 'bird watching', a term which he himself coined. (William Barnes, coincidentally, was the originator of the term 'bird lore'.) Selous was a modest and self-effacing man who made a close and continuous study of birds in Britain and parts of Europe, specialising in their varied courtship habits. A Darwinian, he noted examples of natural selection and species survival in his reports.

Selous had begun by killing birds for study, but by 1898 had come to regard this method of collecting specimens as undesirable, as he explained in his *Bird Watching* of 1901: 'For myself, I must confess that I once belonged to this great, poor army of killers, though, happily, a bad shot, a most *fatigable* collector, and a poor, half-hearted bungler, generally. But now that I have watched birds closely, the killing of them seems to me as something monstrous and horrible...'

In this belief he differed from his older and more famous brother Frederick, big game hunter and model for the character Allan Quartermain in several of Rider Haggard's colonial-era novels, notably *King Solomon's Mines*. Frederick's exploits were typical of his age; a kind of thoughtless zeal for collection which hastened the extinction of many animals, birds and plants – though it should be added that many of his trophies were presented to public collections, notably the Natural History Museum, where there is a memorial to him in the main entrance hall. His was a natural history of destruction.

The effects of such activities on the Devonshire seashore was witnessed by the writer Edmund Gosse, son of a naturalist, and described in his autobiography *Father and Son*, 1907. As a child he had seen the unspoiled beauty of the shore, 'the great prawns gliding like transparent launches, *anthea* waving in the twilight its thick white waxen tentacles, and the fronds of the dulse faintly streaming in the water, like huge red banners in some reverted atmosphere.' He mourned the subsequent loss of his 'Garden of Eden':

> All this is long over, and done with. The ring of living beauty drawn about our shores was a very thin and fragile one. It had existed all those centuries solely in consequence of the indifference, the blissful ignorance of man. These rock-basins, fringed by corallines, filled

> with still water almost as pellucid as the upper air itself, thronged with beautiful sensitive forms of life – they exist no longer, they are all profaned, and emptied, and vulgarised. An army of 'collectors' has passed over them, and ravaged every corner of them.

The damage was irreparable. The increasing use of photography as a record reduced the plunder, but many species had already disappeared.

*

Selous watched birds from his own garden in Wyke, as his grandson George Cobbett remembered. 'There was a hut at the bottom of the long garden where Grandpa used to sit and watch birds. It was a real West Country place and there were stone walls with ferns growing on them and there would be the moist smells of cows and camomile and a clanking of pails in the nearby dairy.' Selous watched birds in Kent and Suffolk, in the Shetland Isles – and back in Dorset. In *Realities of Bird Life*, 1927, he describes the mutual behaviour of peewits and black-headed gulls there, which he had observed in 1902, on 'these wind-swept, almost spray-swept downs'. He had watched peewits before; the black-headed gulls were new to him. The gulls, in acts of 'piracy', stole food from the peewits, which seemed to acquiesce in the thefts, as if the gulls had some right to behave in this way. Observations such as this one were fresh and original; Selous also wrote well and evocatively. His specimens fly free like the swans from his pages: they are not doomed to be stuffed forever in mahogany cases.

Selous' books were much respected. He dedicated *Realities of Bird Life* to Thomas Hardy, and in a previously unpublished letter of September 27th 1927, the eighty-seven-year-old author replied:

> I find myself in possession of a handsome & interesting book which I owe to your generosity.
>
> Many thanks for it. I have not got far into it yet, but far enough to discover what an extraordinarily close & minute acquaintance you have with the bird people. I was born in the country, and lived there in my youth – quite, in fact, among wild birds, & yet I never learnt half the things about them that you know.
>
> The book has, I believe, only lately come out, & I hope there will be as good a demand for it as there ought to be.
>
> Yours sincerely
> *Thomas Hardy*
>
> P.S. I don't deserve the kind inscription at the beginning! T.H.

A modest man, Hardy is understating his knowledge of ornithology and his innate empathy with all living creatures. He hated cruelty to them, especially the shooting of game birds, which were 'brought into being by artificial means', for that purpose alone. In his finest novel, *Tess of the d'Urbervilles*, the abandoned Tess takes shelter for the night in a plantation. She makes 'a sort of nest' in the dry dead leaves, but sleep comes to her only fitfully, a sleep disturbed by unfamiliar sounds. 'Sometimes it was a palpitation, sometimes a flutter; sometimes it was a sort of gasp or gurgle. Soon she was certain that the noises came from wild creatures of some kind, the more so when, originating in the boughs overhead, they were followed by the fall of a heavy body upon the ground.'

At daybreak, as soon as light dawns in the little wood, Tess begins to look around her. 'Under the trees several pheasants lay about, their rich plumage dabbled with blood; some were dead, some feebly twitching a wing, some staring up at the sky, some pulsating quickly, some contorted, some stretched out – all of them writhing in agony, except the fortunate ones whose tortures had ended during the night by the inability of nature to bear more.' For Tess, the sufferings of the pheasants put her own misery into perspective; Hardy treats both woman and birds with a tender pity.

*

A stealthier way of luring birds to their deaths was with the use of a duck decoy.

Oh, what have you got for dinner, Mrs Bond?
There's beef in the larder, and ducks on the pond.
Oh, dilly dilly, dilly dilly, come and be killed.
For you must be stuffed, and my customers filled.

A simple but deadly device, the duck decoy has been a feature of Abbotsbury Swannery for over 350 years, ever since Sir John Strangways leased the land to John Hearne of

Sherborne in 1655, a man who proceeded to have one built at his own expense. The Abbotsbury decoy's design has scarcely changed over the centuries, and it is now the oldest of its kind among the few examples which survive.

Though most decoys were to be found in East Anglia, there was another Dorset example on the heath-lands of the Charborough Park estate near Morden, close enough to Poole Harbour to attract some of its many birds inland. This decoy, on a reach of water surrounded by trees, was visited by Daniel Defoe during his tour of England in 1724–26. He observed with relish the accompanying traps, set 'to preserve [it] from vermin, polecats, kites and such-like'. Beside the traps was a gibbet 'where abundance of such creatures taken were hang'd up for show'. While he was there a 'monstrous eagle' was caught in one of the traps and beaten to death, This cruel act caused the landowner much dismay, as he could otherwise have put the live bird – rare in the southern counties – on display, or else sold it on to another gentleman.

Morden decoy was abandoned after 1856, though the pond and decoy house are still there, in what is now a nature reserve. The decoy fell out of use because the ever-increasing noise of shooting close by distracted the wild fowl from settling on the pond. For the trickery to work, peace and quiet were needed.

Until the mid-seventeenth century, decoys had been rather primitive constructions, using nets to encircle a stretch of water. The nets met in a V-shaped point, which was attached to a tunnel, down which the ducks were led or driven into bags at the end (which was also their end). The decoys could only be used at times when the birds were grounded: that is, during the moulting season, or when they were still unfledged chicks. It has been suggested that the word decoy comes from the Dutch *endekooy* which means 'duck-cage'. This is a likely explanation, as the Dutch were the original inventors of the decoy system.

Early attempts were made to restrict the numbers of birds trapped in this way when it was discovered that some varieties were becoming scarce. In 1534 an Act was passed 'to avoid destroying of Wild Fowl' by forbidding the activity between the first of May and the end of August. The birds' eggs, too, were protected under the Act.

The later system was more elaborate. A quiet spot was chosen, protected by trees and shrubs. There was a standard layout. Within the trees was a pond, shaped like an open handkerchief, with curved narrow ditches known as 'pipes' radiating from each corner. These were covered with nets, supported by wooden rods. A plan of the Swannery's decoy, dating from 1804, shows all four pipes in operation; though now only two are used, the eastern one being the 'Fleet pipe'. (The south-eastern corner pipe were abandoned in the 1950s after the adjoining screen was burnt down.)

Side screens allowed the decoy man to spy on the unsuspecting ducks as they approached the pipe. Taller than any man, the screens had spaces between them, linked by low fences over which a dog could jump. (Dogs have not been used in Abbotsbury since the early 20th century.) The dogs chosen for this work were usually small, reddish brown and bushy-tailed, resembling the foxes who frequent the decoys and which are much feared by ducks. Dogs were employed when food was plentiful elsewhere, making the decoy less of an attraction to passing birds. Judas ducks are also used to lure the birds into swimming on into the tunnel. The slight curve of the pipes means that they cannot see the fate of their fellows at their final destination. Once they are securely in the pipe, the decoy man appears. The ducks take fright, and rush into the bag at the pipe's end.

The word 'duck' suggests the white-feathered, orange-beaked farmyard birds, which are often portrayed paddling placidly on nursery rhyme ponds – but many other wild fowl are lured into the traps. They include teal, mallard, widgeon, and pochard. The first Ilchester estate record on the subject, dated 1662, showed that 112 ducks and teal were sent to the kitchens of the Strangways house at Melbury, near Evershot, and another 966 were sold.

By 1659 John Hearne of Sherborne had died, and the decoy became the property of the Strangways family. The family owned yet another decoy at Compton Dundon near Glastonbury, built by Thomas Strangways in 1695, and further protein was supplied by the birds in the dovecote – the 'Pigeon House' to the east of Abbotsbury Tithe Barn, which dates from monastic times.

Since 1937, the birds found in the decoy have been ringed. This practice began with teal and mallard, and continued with many other wild fowl. As well as the ringing, the birds are sexed and measured – and released back into the wild. In their book *Abbotsbury & the Swannery*, swanherds John Fair and Don Moxom describe the joys of this work.

Decoying duck on the edge of the Fleet at Abbotsbury is one of the pleasures of winter, be it at dawn in the face of a chilling easterly or with rain beating in from the south-west under a darkening sky. Ringing and releasing helps us to learn more about how best to help these colourful elegant birds survive the problems that now confront them, so that we in turn can look forward to many more centuries of 'working the pipes' of the Abbotsbury decoy.

Abbotsbury Alibi

A Gypsy Story

Towards the end of 1752, three Gypsies arrived at the Red Lion, South Perrott, on the borders of Dorset and Somerset. They were a mother, Mary Squires, and her son and daughter, George and Lucy. Mary Squires herself was a curious figure, once seen, never forgotten. An elderly woman, she was tawny-faced, tall and vigorous, if somewhat bowed. She was fond of smoking a pipe. Her most noticeable feature however was her gargoyle-like, protruding under-lip, 'as big almost as 'a little child's arm' – or so it was later said.

Her son George was also tall, he sported a wig and a great-coat, and was very much in charge. His sister Lucy, though as dark-skinned as the rest of her family, was described as looking very unlike a Gypsy. All three had very little luggage, and did not carry a tent with them, preferring to stay under a roof rather than the stars. George carried a pedlar's pack, and the three seemed to be carrying a sufficient amount of money between them.

The trio could be vague about their comings and goings – dates, other than those of festivals and fairs, were not often important to Gypsies. Their later testimonies about their movements were complicated by the country's change

Etching of Mary Squires 'on her Examination before Justice Fielding' 1753

that year from the 'Old Style' Julian calendar to the 'New Style' Gregorian one, in line with the rest of Europe. This change seemed to some people to have caused a loss of eleven days. It certainly created a lot of confusion.

Once in Dorset, the Gypsies travelled from inn to inn, establishments which have now vanished, or at the very least have been renamed. In their wandering way, the family were making for Abbotsbury. Always uncertain of their reception in a region, Gypsies in Dorset were more commonly found on the wide northern reaches of Cranborne Chase. In neighbouring Hampshire they frequented the New Forest where, like the deer, they could remain undetected among the trees. Gypsies had (and still have) a hard time of it, being generally regarded as undesirable vagrants. Occasionally, though mostly in literature, they are portrayed as a kind of noble savage, closer and more attuned to nature and the land than their house-dwelling compatriots. The truth lies somewhere between these two extremes. Geoffrey Grigson in his *Shell Country Alphabet* pithily summed them up as 'an unlettered race of quiet, rather mildly cuckooish independence'. Their problem was their difference, their desire to live on their own terms.

On December 30th the three Gypsies reached the Three Horseshoes at Wynyard's Gap, where they had a meal of beer, bread and cheese. They did not seem to attract any hostility as they travelled, which suggests they were familiar figures. From Wynyard's Gap they went on to an inn at Litton Cheney, where they heard the church bells ring in the New Year. They finally reached Abbotsbury and the Old Ship inn on New Year's Day (Old Style). Here they stayed for nine days among the revellers: the inn must have been a spacious one, and more than just an alehouse. They appeared to have felt very much at home in Abbotsbury, because Lucy Squires was being courted by a local shoemaker, William Clarke. The reason they would give for leaving the village was the news that Polly, another daughter of Mary Squires, had been taken ill in London (though how they had managed to receive this news is a mystery). While in Abbotsbury they began to run out of money, and George sold some of the haberdashery in his pack. Mary Squires, meanwhile, spent her time by the fire, smoking her pipe and telling the occasional fortune.

With all this wandering from alehouse to inn, the Gypsies knew that they risked punishment for being 'rogues and vagabonds'. An estate village could be a conveniently private hideout. The lords of the manor were living away and out of sight in their great house at Melbury Sampford, several miles to the north. The villagers were sometimes left to their own devices – and local inns, too, might be independent of the estates they served.

The Gypsies left Abbotsbury for more exposed, riskier places. The next night they stayed at the Chequers in Portesham, then made their way up to London, arriving around January 20th. Once there, they stayed in Enfield Wash, in a bawdy-house belonging to a certain Mother Wells. Another of the occupants, it was afterwards claimed, was a young servant girl named Elizabeth Canning, and on February 1st both Susannah Wells and Mary Squires were arrested and charged with assaulting her. In addition, the Gypsy was accused of 'stealing, taking away from her person one pair of stays, value 10s'. The stays – boned corsets, laced at the back – were valuable enough to make the theft a hanging offence.

Elizabeth Canning's short life had so far been a very respectable one. She was eighteen years old, plump, and pitted with smallpox scars. She worked as a scullery-maid, and lived with her mother and three younger siblings in Aldermanbury in the City of London. Then, on New Year's Day, dressed in her holiday finery and carrying her Christmas money, she abruptly disappeared. She returned just as suddenly a month later on January 29th, the day before the third anniversary of the execution of King Charles I (a memorable date for the country). She was thin, bruised and threadbare, and claimed that she had been kidnapped by two men. Liable to fits, she suffered a blackout during her snatching, and came to consciousness to find herself in the bawdy-house, where Squires cut off her stays (a symbol of her respectability) and where attempts were made, she said, to starve her into becoming a whore. These efforts she resisted.

Her plight soon attracted much public sympathy. When she repeated her charges before the magistrate, who happened to be the blind novelist Henry Fielding, her case seemed unassailable. A blameless young girl, she had been imprisoned by a grotesque old woman – a Gypsy at that – and by a brothel-keeper. Fielding himself believed her to be innocent, taken against her will to what he described in his pamphlet 'A Clear State of the Case of Elizabeth Canning' as 'a little hedge bawdy house'.

This pamphlet was the first of many similar publications. Lilian de la Tour, in her own contribution to the Canning controversy, a dramatic retelling of events entitled *Elizabeth is Missing, the rich and raffish story of the four weeks' disappearance of Elizabeth Canning* (1947) lists thirteen pamphlets published between March and July 1753, plus another twenty-one published between May and November 1754, at the time of the retrial. Many more articles and books followed over the years, and continue to be produced. The case is one of endless fascination and speculation.

Squires and Wells were promptly found guilty, despite the former pleading as an alibi that she was in Abbotsbury at the time of Canning's alleged abduction. Wells was sentenced to branding on the thumb – a sentence which was carried out immediately – while the old Gypsy was sentenced to death and imprisoned in Newgate to await her punishment.

Though public opinion was vociferously against them, not everyone believed in the two women's guilt. The Lord Mayor of London, Sir Crisp Gascoyne, pursued the case, and Canning was charged with perjury. James Harris, vicar of Abbotsbury, wrote in support of the Gypsies, while fifteen prominent villagers sent a second letter, and six people signed an affidavit. More remarkably, thirty-seven people from Abbotsbury came forward to support Mary Squires's alibi. Many of these people may never have left their home county before, or even their village. Their actions were brave because, as well as the expense of travel, they were taking a risk. Two Abbotsbury witnesses had come forward at the first trial: John Gilbert, landlord of the Old Ship, and Lucy's loyal suitor William Clarke. They were accompanied by a third man, Thomas Greville, landlord of The Lamb in Coombe Bissett, an inn in where the Gypsies stayed when they left Abbotsbury. After the verdict in favour of Canning they had all been charged with 'wilful corrupt perjury', though they were later acquitted. Worse still, Thomas Greville died of smallpox, which he had contracted in the court.

As a result of their actions, Canning was found guilty and sentenced to seven years' transportation to the American colonies. The case had been complicated, involving a cast of about one hundred and fifty people. A gaggle of witnesses came forward on Canning's behalf, not all of them truthful. Some changed their evidence. Others had not actually witnessed anything at all. There were charges and counter charges, and it is unlikely that either the accused or their accuser (or their witnesses) were telling the whole truth. The question remains; what were Canning and Squires actually doing at the crucial time? Could Elizabeth Canning have been pregnant, disappearing to have an abortion or to give birth secretly? Did she spend the lost time with a lover who turned against her? While there is no doubt that Mary Squires was in Abbotsbury when Canning vanished, what purpose was she there for, other than giving her daughter Lucy the opportunity to see her lover?

The Gypsy family were already well-known to some of the inhabitants, and had been accepted by them. In his book on the case, Harvey Darton suggests that they were members of a smuggling gang and that Abbotsbury could have been part of their regular route. If the Gypsies were their fellow smugglers, this would explain the enormous amount of support they received from Abbotsbury residents – and the amount of money they had at their disposal. There were mysterious gaps in the account of their journey: they were unable to remember the time before they entered Dorset at South Perrott, or exactly when they were around Basingstoke. One of the plethora of pamphlets suggested that 'All the people at Abbotsbury, including even the Vicar, are Fortune-Tellers, Impostors, Bawds, Whores, Thieves, Robbers, Smugglers, Murderers and Plunderers of Shipwrecks.'

There was of course much smuggling in Abbotsbury, as there was in all the villages hidden away behind Chesil Bank. Even the Strangways were not averse. In the 1720s Thomas Strangways had claimed a cache of contraband wine and brandy as his 'right of wreck', saying that the find was in fact salvaged from a lost ship. It is quite likely that the Gypsies were smuggling – though it should be noted that one witness who came forward for the defence in the first trial was Andrew Wake, excise officer of Abbotsbury.

*

Frederick Joseph Harvey Darton, an expert on children's books, had an intense love for the English countryside – especially Dorset, which he discovered while he was a student. In his *Marches of Wessex*, written over the course of twenty years, he travelled through time across the county. He walked from place to place, experiencing for himself the varieties of the landscape. When writing this book, his first with Dorset as its subject, he came across the Canning case, which he discussed at some length. Then, in 1936, he published an entire book about it.

For *Alibi Pilgrimage* Darton rambled his way from South Perrott, across Dorset and as far as London, in a dogged attempt to follow the trail of the three Gypsies. He traced out a route by footpath and stile, bush and briar, along now near-forgotten roads, a route illustrated with his own quaintly-drawn maps. 'Old tracks', he wrote, 'are the true archives of the country'. Waylaid by the landscape, his descriptions are so painstakingly detailed that he sometimes seems to forget the ostensible object of his book. For him the journey mattered as much as the arrival.

Two years before his death Darton moved to Cerne Abbas, where he stayed in the Red Lion inn. While there, he produced a detailed study of aspects of village life called *English Fabric*, with many examples taken from Cerne itself.

Harvey Darton is buried in the churchyard by the old abbey, under a stout stone cross.

Darton believed in the Gypsies' alibi, as have most of the later commentators. Truth – or the search for it – has also ventured into fiction. In her novel *The Franchise Affair* (1948) Josephine Tey has no doubt that Mary Squires was innocent. Her twentieth century heroine, Marion Sharpe, a tall, Gypsyish-looking woman, lives in genteel poverty with her tetchy white-haired old mother in a lonely house called The Franchise. They are accused by a fifteen-year-old schoolgirl, Betsy Kane, of abduction and ill-use. While following the pattern of the trial, with Betty as the butter-wouldn't-melt young victim, the expert story-telling is marred by the book's relentless snobbery: the Sharpes's blue blood eventually triumphs over the bad blood of Betty, the adopted child of a feckless mother.

The real Elizabeth Canning was transported to Wethersfield in Connecticut where she lived, as a member of the family, in the house of the Reverend Rector-Colonel, Elisha Williams, a prominent Methodist. She had been lucky in her placing: her supporters had seen to that – though even here she managed to attract attention to herself by publicly describing one of her dreams. She claimed she dreamt that while 'being employed at her Needle, there appeared before her, a venerable old Matron in a high crown's Hat, and antique Garb, informing her that her name was Shipton'. Mother Shipton, by day the prophetess of Knaresborough, apparently advised her to follow in the footsteps of Joan of Arc, though on behalf of the English rather than the French. In consequence (her dream was as muddled as night visions commonly are) her eternal enemy, Mary Squires, would be burnt to death. This episode inspired yet another pamphlet, *Virtue Triumphant,* an account of her life in exile written by yet another devotee of Canning. Reverting to convention, in 1756 Elizabeth Canning married and produced five children. She was to spend the rest of her life in America.

And as for Mary, George and Lucy Squires, nothing more is known of their lives. They disappeared from the cruel limelight as silently as they had entered it, and were never remarked on again. It seems unlikely that they ever returned to Abbotsbury, whose villagers were the merciful providers of their alibi.

Village for Sale

On March 15th 1954, in the hall of Winchester Castle, an even more notorious trial began. Three men stood in the dock, accused of 'conspiracy to incite certain male persons to commit serious offences with male persons'. The three men were Edward Barrington Douglas-Scott-Montagu, better known as Lord Montagu of Beaulieu, Peter Wildeblood, Diplomatic Correspondent of the *Daily Mail* (then a rather different newspaper) and Major Michael Augustus Lane-Fox Pitt-Rivers, heir to the Pitt-Rivers estates in Wiltshire and Dorset. At his trial in 1895 Oscar Wilde had been charged with 'gross indecency'; this 1950s trial caused as much scandal as its Victorian predecessor.

There was, however, one telling difference. In the case of Wilde, the authorities had been reluctant to pursue the charges, and gave him the opportunity to escape, which – for whatever reason – he refused to do. In the case of Montagu, Wildeblood and Pitt-Rivers they were determined to continue the prosecution to its bitter end.

In the 1950s, homosexuality was still illegal and anyone discovered in such acts, even in private, would be liable to prosecution leading to a term of at least seven years imprisonment. Homophobia was at a peak, and the police –

particularly after the appointment in 1953 of Sir John Nott-Bower as Commissioner of the Metropolitan Police – were ruthless in identifying (and often trapping) anyone who attracted their suspicions. Around the same time, the Home Secretary, Sir David Maxwell Fyfe, another hardliner, called for 'a new drive against male vice'.

Public figures had become a target. In 1952 Alan Turing, breaker of the Enigma Code, had been found guilty of homosexual acts. Forced to undergo hormone treatment, he committed suicide in 1954. In 1953, the Shakespearian actor John Gielgud was found guilty of cottaging in a public lavatory and fined for the offence. His theatre audiences were undeterred by this, and his career unaffected, but the experience damaged his health.

The main target of the March 1954 case was its most famous and popular figure, Lord Montagu of Beaulieu. Montagu had already been in court the previous year – in what was in effect a show trial – charged with an indecent attack on two boy scouts at a beach he owned on his Beaulieu estate. This was a charge he continued to deny, and for which he was found not guilty. Now he was in court again, on another serious charge.

The Beaulieu beach hut where the alleged assault had taken place also featured in the 1954 trial. Montagu offered the use of the hut for the August Bank Holiday week to Peter Wildeblood, Wildeblood's lover Eddie McNally, and McNally's fellow airman John Reynolds. In his scrupulous book on the case, *Against the Law*, published in 1955, Wildeblood described this holiday home as 'a Spartan, two-room building to which water had to be brought in milk-churns'.

On their first evening, Montagu and some of his guests joined them on the beach. Wildeblood commented that 'The party which followed has achieved more notoriety than any other since the days of Nero, but I am bound to confess that it was, in fact, extremely dull'.

Wildeblood was cheered when, as the weather looked unpromising for the rest of the week, Michael Pitt-Rivers (who was Montagu's second cousin, and was visiting to discuss business matters) invited the three men to stay at King John's House, a hunting-lodge on his Tollard Royal estate in North Dorset. The estate included the Larmer Tree pleasure grounds, which contain a charmingly eclectic collection of buildings: Indian houses, a bandstand, an open-air theatre, a Greek temple and a lake with Japanese bronze storks, all erected by Michael's great-grandfather, the archaeologist and ethnologist General Augustus Henry Lane-Fox Pitt-Rivers, for the education and entertainment of the masses. At nearby Farnham, there was a further attraction in the Dorset branch of the Pitt-Rivers Museum of Antiquities.

Their stay at the Larmer Tree was, Wildeblood wrote, 'a very happy experience'.

> I [could] explore the museum and get on with my writing; the two airmen could make themselves useful by helping to clear the grounds, which were overgrown with brambles and weeds.

But the outcome of this peaceful holiday was far less happy. In January 1954, (after Montagu had been acquitted of the first offence in December) the London homes of

Wildeblood, Montagu and Pitt-Rivers were searched without warrant (and in the absence of the latter two men). Wildeblood was not allowed to contact his solicitor, and was obliged to make a statement without his presence. (He did not see a legal representative until after the police had broken the news of the arrest of the three public figures to the Press.)

McNally and Reynolds were frightened and tricked into giving evidence for the prosecution, while the prosecuting council appeared amazed that men from such different social classes had chosen to associate. The three accused denied all charges. Then Wildeblood was asked, point-blank, whether or not he was a homosexual. Fully realising that his answer might ruin his career and reputation – and that he was running the risk of a very long prison sentence – he courageously replied, 'Yes'.

Montagu, Wildeblood and Pitt-Rivers were all found guilty. Wildeblood and Pitt-Rivers were sentenced to eighteen month in prison, and Montagu to twelve months. As they left the court, they prepared to meet the routinely hostile crowd, but somehow, something had changed. Wildeblood wrote:

> …the crowd began to press around us, shouting. It was some moments before I realised that they were not shouting insults, but words of encouragement. They tried to pat us on the back and told us to 'keep smiling', and when the doors were shut they went on talking through the windows and gave the thumbs-up sign and clapped their hands.

Public opinion was beginning to change. In 1954 the Wolfenden Committee was set up to discuss possible amendments to the law. Three homosexual men contributed to the consultation, including Peter Wildeblood, who had written from prison for permission to become involved. The other two gay contributors gave evidence anonymously; only Wildeblood spoke in his own name.

The Report recommended that 'homosexual behaviour between consenting adults in private should no longer be a criminal offence', and this became law with the Sexual Offences Act of 1967. The trial of Montagu, Wildeblood and Pitt-Rivers had been a major factor in the setting up of the inquiry and its outcome. It also had another, much more unexpected effect.

In 1958 Michael's father, Captain George Henry Lane-Fox Pitt-Rivers, put the whole of his Burton Bradstock estate up for auction. The cover of the fat, cream-coloured catalogue (an expensive item in itself, costing ten shillings) described the sale as comprising:

> Most of This Attractive Village
> Over 3 Miles of Coastline of Unsurpassed Beauty
> Some of Chesil Beach and West Bay.

Among his estates (and it was said that at one time he could have walked from one side of the county to the other without leaving them) Burton Bradstock was a family favourite. During the 1880s they had built two houses, Alpha and Omega, above the shore – Cliff Villas – to use as summer residences. (A bungalow called Grey Stones was added in the 1930s.) In 1927 Cliff Villas was listed by *Kelly's Directory* as the home of George's father, Alexander Pitt-Rivers. After his death, his widow moved into the old coastguard station (which had been used as holiday cottages since its closure in 1907), converting the buildings into a single property. She kept pure-bred chickens 'on a large scale; the methods way ahead of the time' and called the main poultry building 'The Palace'.

Burton Bradstock was a place the family regarded with affection, so it seemed strange that they should choose to sell that particular village among all their holdings. There had been a precedent in 1919, when the Cerne Abbas section of the Pitt-Rivers estate was sold at auction to pay off heavy death duties (Harvey Darton, admirer of the village, attended the sale in dismay) but in 1958 there did not appear to be any such financial imperative.

There was, it seems, a more personal reason. Captain George was not a father likely to sympathise with his eldest son's bitter experiences. He was a man of extreme views. Wounded in the First World War, he became a distinguished anthropologist, and a member of the Eugenics Society (Eugenics is defined by the Oxford Dictionary as 'the science of improving a population by controlled breeding to increase the occurrence of desirable heritable characteristics'. 'Improvement' could include compulsory sterilisation of people regarded as unfit for breeding.) In the 1930s he became leader of the Wessex Agricultural Defence Association, which campaigned against the tithe system. He stood as an independent in the 1935 General Election, coming second to last. Through this campaign, he met Oswald Mosley, head of the British Union of Fascists, and invited him to the family manor house at Hinton St Mary. He gave shelter to William Joyce, who became notorious as 'Lord Haw-Haw' when broadcasting propaganda from Germany during the Second World War. In 1937 Pitt-Rivers went to Germany to attend the Nuremberg Rally and met Adolf Hitler. He opposed the billeting of city children in rural Dorset. (His opinions, as Patrick Wright has observed, were 'a bizarre mixture of the utterly localised and the grand swoop'.)

The authorities, however, took his political activities so seriously that in 1940 he was detained under Defence Regulation 18B and placed in the Elephant House at Bertram Mills Circus's winter quarters on Ascot racecourse. (How the elephants reacted to their lodger is not recorded.) The internment camp, number 007, was swathed in sombre pines, and held about six hundred people, most of them foreign nationals. George Pitt-Rivers was released under surveillance in 1942, but was not allowed to return to Dorset until the war was over.

Now, for his own reasons, he was selling his estate at Burton Bradstock, an estate that included almost the entire village (along with land to the east of the river in West Bay) and the first part of Chesil Bank. The auctioneers were Senior and Godwin of Sturminster Newton.

As there were 144 lots, the sale took place over two days, from July 31st to August 1st 1958. It was held in a marquee in the field next to the village's recreation ground. The original venue had been the Women's Institute Hall, but that proved altogether too small.

The estate's tenants had been alerted beforehand by a letter from George Pitt-Rivers. He wrote that he could no longer continue to subsidise the estate 'without the prospect, as I had originally planned, of any happy succession in my family'. (Pitt-Rivers' decision was not, however, as sudden as it might have seemed to the villagers. At least ten lots were offered with planning permission for development.)

Not surprisingly, anxious villagers packed the tent, shoulder to shoulder with speculative outsiders. Many of the local people did not fully understand about mortgages, and had never borrowed money before. Their tenancies were often held by verbal agreement, and rents were low. Feeling powerless, some of them did not even attempt to bid, but watched helplessly as their properties fell rapidly under the hammer. 'A feature of the sale was its speed', the *Western Gazette* reported. 'On the first day 75 lots were sold in two and a half hours – possibly a record for a property sale'. Captain Pitt-Rivers himself was absent, he was said to be away in London.

In her book *Two Days One Summer*, a comprehensive account of the auction is given by Elizabeth Buckler Gale – a native of Burton Bradstock and the village's local historian – who herself witnessed the hectic events of 1958. She noted that those tenants who bid for their properties on the first day were successful, which was a great relief to the villagers. There was also a 'mystery buyer' whose agent was Mr John Jeffery of Donhead. Jeffery secured ten lots: Manor Farm; an accommodation field 'fronting Barr Road' (a potential building site); Cogden Farm; and three lots of land fronting Bredy Road; plus another 17 acres opposite Bredy

Farm; and 'Batten's Ground', which consisted of more land adjoining Barr Road. His final pair of purchases were of the main and eastern parts of the West Dorset Golf Course, totalling ninety-three acres in all, situated above the sea at West Bay.

Other lots had already been withdrawn; four had been sold to Bridport Rural District Council, and the Parish Council was negotiating for purchase of the village allotments. The Wesleyan Chapel was gifted to its Trustees by George Pitt-Rivers and the village reading-room given to the British Legion. A number of other, more important lots had also been withdrawn – secured before the auction by the mystery buyer.

At the commencement of the sale, Mr Ingram the auctioneer had emphasised the rich potential for development of the village. Anything was possible. He pointed out that the seaside town of Bournemouth had been 'a tiny village a hundred years ago'. R B Howarth, chairman of the Parish Council, disagreed with this prediction. He announced that 'steps have been taken to prevent any indiscriminate development. Development will be controlled, and that applies particularly to the coastal area, which I hope to see preserved intact'.

It was noticeable that many of the lots purchased by the mystery buyer and his agent were of land close to the coast, or of other land most vulnerable to development. Among the most important was lot 83, described as:

'Burton Beach and the Hive. An Important Development Property, mostly with Vacant Possession. 32 acres, including over a mile of beach, Car Park and Café, with Valuable

Accommodation Land.' This lot included the lucrative toll road down to the beach, the rights to shingle extraction, the café and the fishermen's green and net shed (which they continued to use). Lot 88, the land above the Hive, was another significant purchase for the mystery buyer.

Almost every lot was sold. Elizabeth Buckler Gale, who was also a witness to the aftermath, described its effects in *Two Days One Summer*. 'The familiar scene in Burton Bradstock of everyone knowing who was who and who rented what from the Estate had been swept away overnight... The link with the Pitt-Rivers family and their ancestors as the landlords, that had existed for some three hundred and fifty years, was over.'

The problems which afflict so many villages (especially those close to the sea or of picturesque appearance) occurred in Burton Bradstock very quickly. After the sale, many of the successful local purchasers struggled to pay their mortgages. Incomers arrived, some of them regarded as being overbearing and patronising to their new country neighbours. Having usually only visited in the summer, they had no inkling of the pattern of life in a working village. There were complaints about the mud and dung, about washing lines and crowing cocks, church bells and tractors and other such everyday disturbances of their eagerly-acquired rural idyll.

There was rapid gentrification. The village was already accustomed to tourism, though only as a minor part of life. In 1906 Frederick Treves in his perambulation of Dorset, had commented on the village's attractiveness, adding that 'the diligent holiday-maker has discovered this spot, and has sown therein the seeds of deterioration'. Now the villagers had to become resigned to holiday cottages which were left empty in the winter, to second homes and to buying for investment which forced up the cost of housing, so that the original inhabitants could no longer afford to live there.

Planning applications came in thick and fast. Within twenty years, the village had doubled in size. Tourism had become its major industry, and today the village is fashionable. The fields each side of the toll-road – built by George Pitt-Rivers down to the shore – are lined with cars. The Hive Beach Café, once a wooden shack, is much larger now and specialises in seafood and other Dorset produce. Above on the cliffs, one of the family villas has become the Seaside Boarding House, with restaurant and bar. Previously called 'Bay View', a family hotel, it had been empty for several years. So haunted did it seem that the film of Stephen King's novel 'The Shining' was screened there, to a full house. (The second villa had already been sold off before the 1958 sale. Under the name Barton Olivers it had been a holiday home for composer Lionel Bart and – or so the story goes – the entertainer Vic Oliver, who was reported as calling Burton Bradstock 'a cemetery without lights'. A more recent owner was the singer and activist Billy Bragg.)

A major attraction is the still unspoilt shoreline. Thanks to the prescience of the mystery buyer and his agent, the beach and its hinterland have been saved from development. (Another party to the conservation was the Burton Bradstock Association, founded shortly after the sale, which acquired Lot 83 and administered it until 1973.)

The mystery buyer was revealed to be none other than Michael Pitt-Rivers, who, in the days before the sale had a

*Reed-cutter on Cogden Mere (*Maurice Ouseley*).*

secret meeting with some of the Burton Bradstock farmers at Cogden Farm. It was, as Elizabeth Buckler Gale remarks, 'an out-of-the-way place and as secluded as could be found for a confidential meeting' since 'the village [was] awash with speculation'. For his part, Michael Pitt-Rivers said that he wanted to 'ensure continuity'. His purchases before and at the sale were of some beautiful and vulnerable lots of land, for which he may have had a fondness since his childhood.

Almost all the coastal strip at Burton Bradstock today belongs to the National Trust. Their Enterprise Neptune Coastline Campaign, which began in 1965, was a bold attempt to save as much of the coastline as possible from the speculative building and urban sprawl which threatened places like Burton Bradstock. In 1967 – a year after his father's death – the Trust acquired 39.31 acres of freehold land at Burton Cliff and Freshwater Bay from Michael

Pitt-Rivers. The rest of the coastal strip (other than the Old Coastguards Caravan site) was acquired between 1973 when the Burton Bradstock Association handed over Lot 83 'for the benefit of the Nation' (as they had always planned to do) and 2014. Burton Cliff was acquired in 1990 and Bind Barrow in 1997. The coastal area has remained undeveloped.

Major Michael Pitt-Rivers retired from the Welsh Guards in 1953. As the elder of the two sons of George and his first wife, an actress whose stage name was Mary Hinton, he already had charge of a great part of the family's Dorset and Wiltshire lands. He was a pioneer conservationist and enthusiast for tree-planting, being responsible, like his Cranborne Chase neighbour Rolf Gardiner, for the planting of three million trees during his lifetime, – an enterprise which began in Burton Bradstock – and he devoted himself to his estates for the rest of his life.

In August 1958, to the mystification of their mutual friends, he married Sonia, the widow and literary guardian of George Orwell. Hilary Spurling, Sonia's biographer, wrote that Sonia had married Pitt-Rivers because she 'believed she could restore Michael to his rightful position in the county by an act of commitment that would provide him, in practical terms, with a hostess while making a public mock of the bigotry and hypercritical intolerance that had singled him out as a high-profile scapegoat under an obsolete law'. However, their union, a *mariage blanc*, fell apart quickly under the strain. Pitt-Rivers's companion for the last forty years of his life was the artist William Gronow Davis, to whom he bequeathed the Larmer Tree Estate, which in 1966 he had described as 'probably the first small 'Country Park', as now envisaged, in the country'.

Michael Pitt-Rivers was the author of the second edition of the *Shell Guide to Dorset* (taking over from Andrew Wordsworth who, 'through lack of time' was mysteriously 'forced to abandon the work for other things'). Pitt-Rivers incorporated some of Wordsworth's notes, but more importantly – as he was following Paul Nash's original edition – he included Nash's fine essay on 'The Face of Dorset', along with many of the artist's surreal photographs and some of his paintings, which Nash had produced wherever he thought no photograph would suffice. This was a highly successful combination.

Pitt-Rivers also included Nash's resounding dedication to the guide:

> To the Landowners of Dorset
> The Council for the Preservation of Rural England
> The Society for the Protection of Ancient Buildings
> And all those courageous enemies of development
> To whom we owe what is left of England.

An Abbotsbury Garland

In 1650, during the Civil War, while he was being kept under curfew by Parliamentarian troops, the staunch Royalist Sir John Strangways wrote a defiant poem which ran to several pages, and included a list of his estates. He had compiled this inventory, he explained, '*since the State hath me denyde/Above five Miles from home to ride,/This note declares the Lands I have,/Which my forefathers to me gave,/Or which for Monie I did buy*'. Among his many estates Abbotsbury, he proclaimed, was the place '*where all the Dwellers in that towne/Me only for their Landlorde own*'.

The Ilchester lands continue to include much of Abbotsbury. Although estate villages – of which Dorset has more than its share – can be seen as something of an anachronism, it may be argued that they still have their uses, as they provide a valuable source of housing for local people. While the after-effects of the 1958 sale of Burton Bradstock rapidly and permanently damaged the village's character, and drove away many long-established families, in 1973 the Ilchester estate chose to take an altogether different direction. In a *Country Life* article of 1975, Brian Dunning commended their decision: 'Rather than sell Abbotsbury piecemeal to the highest bidder, they chose to let buildings on long leases, subject to very rigorous control by the estate. Architects were commissioned to produce a comprehensive development plan. The report is a classic. Nothing escaped their attention.'

In her preface to the survey, Lady Theresa Agnew wrote that although her family still owned most of the village 'the days have gone' when they could provide much of the employment. But they could supply the housing and maintain its standards. Thus, as well as studying the social aspects of village life, the architectural features 'which play a great part in giving the village its special character' were also studied in great detail, street by street and sometimes house by house.

In the village plan such eyesores as concrete garages and galvanised iron fences were condemned, and the importance of respecting both the local styles and proportions of the buildings were emphasised in the monthly meetings on planning matters. Even the wild flowers growing in the walls were documented, as were the butterflies on the grassy verges. The village was examined not in a piecemeal fashion, but in its entirety.

One of the results of this approach was that Abbotsbury remains visually very pleasing. There's an absence of some of those trappings of individuality which can make or mar other villages: the picture windows, plastic doors and ornate coaching lamps which are used to bring a fresh character to over-restored dwellings.

Its appearance is one of the features which draws in the tourists, although Abbotsbury has many other attractions. As well as the Swannery, the Abbey ruins and the Subtropical Gardens, there is a tithe barn and children's farm.

The long main street is well-supplied with tearooms, gift shops and galleries. Tourism is vital to Abbotsbury's economy, just as it is to that of Burton Bradstock, and everywhere it is a mixed blessing. During the season there are traffic jams along Abbotsbury's main thoroughfare, and these are likely to be exacerbated by the thoughtless reductions in the local bus services. Extra cars bring more pollution, and more and more space is acquired for their parking.

This modern state of affairs would have been impossible to envisage in 1924 when the ecologist Rolf Gardiner first visited Abbotsbury. He had come in search of D H Lawrence, whose writings he admired, especially those which raged against the machine. He was disappointed to discover that Lawrence had never actually arrived in the village, and was now far away in New Mexico. He thought that John Middleton Murry, although hospitable, was a poor substitute for his hero, and left hastily the following morning, after a dip in the sea. Gardiner returned in 1928, a time 'when the great elms leading to the Swannery blew down in a phenomenal gale'. He camped in the garden of the Grove, which was occupied by the uncle of his friend the Swanherd, Fred Lexster. He found Abbotsbury to be an idyllic place, 'unperturbed by tourists and traffic'.

> How marvellous was Abbotsbury at that period. Farming was in the depths of the depression, and southern England was an uncultivated green parkland run wild and swamped by weeds and rabbits. Yet at Abbotsbury the historic past was married to an unequalled geological abundance, the strata of many rich soils

> lying in bands from the ridgeline down to the Fleet and the Chesil Bank. Rural life had subsided into dreaminess and passivity. The land was full of ghosts and nostalgia.

In 1924 Gardiner's composer uncle Balfour had bought Gore Farm, on Cranborne Chase, which, after the break-up of some great estates, was in much the same neglected condition as the land around Abbotsbury. With advice from the Forestry Commission, Balfour Gardiner began to plant trees, a project continued by his nephew when the farm was made over to him in 1927 (and which he rebuilt in 1928 after a fire which destroyed all the outbuildings). Rolf Gardiner had been trained in silviculture at Dartington Hall, and, initially together with his uncle, planted about three million trees over the course of the next forty years. In 1933 Rolf Gardiner acquired the Springhead estate at Fontmell Magna from the artist Harold Squire, a member of the London Group of painters. Squire had purchased Springhead in the 1926 Glyn Sale of the Fontmell Magna Estate, and he and his gardener Harold Woolridge had struggled hard for four years to tame this wilderness, until unexpected financial ruin forced him reluctantly to sell up.

At Springhead, Gardiner's wife Marabel continued to create a garden with Harold Woolridge, aided by a few basic tools. Within this garden setting, Marabel organised festivals and wrote plays, in a giddy Merrie English world of folk-song, morris dancing and maypoles. Rolf ran the estate and was in charge of the tree-planting. He organised work camps to which enthusiasts came from all over Europe. Another great tree-planter, Michael Pitt-Rivers, attended some of these camps as a young man. In 1995 he recalled them 'with affection and a little amazement'. It was the era of the Hitler Youth, and other paramilitary groups, so activities like some of those at Springhead (there was reveille at 6.30 am, tent inspections and marching) were generally regarded with a little unease. But there was no question about the value of the tree-planting. In his autobiography, John Stewart Collis tells of the great happiness and satisfaction he felt when working as a forester for Gardiner. He was rewarded when 'Rolf entered this area of about twelve acres, in the Books of the Estate as COLLIS PIECE, and by that name it is now known'.

Meanwhile, at Abbotsbury in 1924 the forester Richard St Barbe Baker founded the Society of Men of the Trees, two years after his creation of the original society in Kenya, where he had been working on tree-planting projects for the Colonial Office.

Abbotsbury may seem an odd place to have chosen for the society's foundation. Although not as bleak as the Isle of Portland, the Chesil coast has a scanty covering of trees, which can scarcely survive the salt winds. Much of the existing woodland has been cultivated. From about 1845, for example, Major W Sparks was planting trees in his manor of Langton Herring. He had found his land to be 'bare of timber, except elm trees', and began by planting scotch firs near Tatton Farm, to the north-east of the village. A further plantation was established opposite Wyke Wood, on the boundary with Abbotsbury, where the scotch firs did not take so well. Neither spruce nor birch could withstand the sea gales any better. *Pinus Austriaca* fir trees, he found, were more suitable. Sparks' largest and perhaps most ambitious plantation was Wans, close to the coastguard station and the old ferry in Langton. He planted Eucalyptus from 'Lord Brougham's beautiful garden' at Cannes – which unsurprisingly was killed by a harsh winter – along with medlars, olives and pampas grass. His trees provided shelter from the wind for cattle, while the felled wood was useful for 'inside work of cottages and other buildings'.

*

Although St Barbe Baker's life had been mostly involved with forestry work overseas, he spent the Second World War years in Dorset. The headquarters of the Men of the Trees, by then in leafy Kensington, was moved to Manor Farm in Puncknowle. Sympathetic to the project, Mrs Palmer, the lady of the manor, waived the first year's rent and put in a bathroom. Annual meetings were held in her house. Baker built a lean-to greenhouse and made 'a large compost heap from old railway sleepers [which] was very soon returning to the land more than was being taken out of it'. He rented a village allotment, where once he temporarily housed 'a few thousand little pine trees' to the alarm of his fellow allotment-holders. He began forestry training courses at Greenleaze, a house up the mud-trampled hill from Manor Farm, which became the wartime headquarters of the Forestry School.

> The training combined theory and practice, starting with twenty minutes' intensive theory each morning, followed by work in the woods or nurseries for the rest of the day. We lived simply in our reed-thatched cottage, 'What shall we have for lunch?' we would say, then go

> out into the garden and get it. In the mackerel fishing season my forestry students might go down to the shore and help with a catch and be invited to take all they needed. Milk and bread were provided by Puncknowle Manor and delivered by the keeper in the course of his rounds.

During the war Baker was also working on national arboreal concerns for the Ministry of Supply, and insisting that 'for every tree felled at least one thousand be planted'. There are still plantations in Puncknowle which were created during the war years: Wall Plantation, beside the aptly named Greenleaze, is close to the site of a Roman building, and there is another plantation on a second Roman site by the Knoll. At the foot of the track which passes Greenleaze a stripling oak, now ivy-clad, has been planted in memory of Richard St Barbe Baker and his woodland work in the district. The accompanying plaque reads:

In tribute to
Richard St Barbe Baker O.B.E.
1889 – 1982
Forester and Conservationist
World wide Ambassador
Founder of "Men of the Trees", now the
"International Tree Foundation"
War-time Headquarters
Forestry School, Greenleaze
Puncknowle
1940–1948

Baker joined the Home Guard while he was working in Puncknowle and in 1946 he married Doreen Long at St Mary's Church there. 'As we left the church', Baker wrote, 'we passed under an arch of spades and axes – the novel idea of the local Home Guard who turned up in full force and afterwards joined the Bishop in the local inn to celebrate.' The couple had two children: Angela born in 1946, and Paul, who was born in 1949 after the family had moved to Gate Farm (more commonly referred to as Wear Farm) next to Abbotsbury Castle. The acquisition of the new farm proved troublesome. A surviving file on the 'Schedule of the Plight of Gate Farm', 1947, contains a lengthy exchange of letters about boundaries and rights-of-way. Baker's future neighbour, a Mr Honeybun, proved obstructive. His objections were based on his claim that 'Capt. Baker employs irresponsible labour, such as Borstal Boys, School boys etc. and allows camping to take place'. Baker was also determined that East Wear Plantation should be included as a part of his tenancy. Trees were more important to him than more conventional modern conveniences.

In 1947 *Spirit of the Trees, an Anthology Inspired by Trees*, with a foreword by Vita Sackville West, was published by the Society at Abbotsbury. All proceeds went to the Tree Planting Fund 'to help restore the ravages of war by replanting'. Tree-planting continued at Langton and around Abbotsbury. In 1973, a plan was produced on behalf of the Campaign for the Preservation of Rural England for a copse on Ashley Chase, just beyond the Wear Farm plantation. On the plan, each individual tree is represented by one of its leaves, painted in autumnal colours. The resulting plantation is a beautiful miniature wood of glossy, variegated trees.

Baker perhaps chose Abbotsbury as a base because, unlike the rest of the Chesil coast, it possesses a rich and diverse collection of trees, planted over the years in the freakish conditions of the Subtropical Gardens. Some of them are visible from the shore. Magnolias, Chinese palms, evergreen holm oaks and an impressive Caucasian wingnut tree are among the many specimens. In 1899, the year the gardens were featured in *Country Life*, Lady Ilchester produced a comprehensive catalogue of over five thousand plants to be found there. The number of varieties had increased enormously due to the enthusiastic contributions of Victorian travellers, who brought back specimens from such far-flung places as China and the Himalayas, contributing to the exotic nature of the gardens.

*

On the encircling hill between Abbotsbury and the shore, the chapel of St Catherine's stands alone. Built as a chantry, of reddish firestone extracted from its hill, the chapel serves as a distinctive sea-mark. Because of its visibility for so many miles across the bay, it escaped destruction during the turbulent Dissolution of the Monasteries. The chapel's position has its disadvantages, being very vulnerable to the weather, and over the years the building has sometimes been in a near-ruinous state. In 1908 Thomas Hardy suggested glazing the windows and putting in doors, which must have helped to preserve the structure. But the chapel has also, and more unusually, acted as the precursor of a dating agency for local girls. In the south doorway there are three 'wishing-holes', into which a hopeful maiden could place her hands and one knee, before chanting an old village rhyme.

> Sweet St Catherine send me a husband.
> A good one I pray.
> But arn-a-one better than narn-a-one
> Oh St Catherine, lend me thine aid,
> And grant I never may die an old maid.

Popular in the Middle Ages, Catherine of Alexandria was the patron saint of virgins, specialising in those in search of husbands. Although she has given her name to the firework, she was not actually martyred on a wheel, as attempts to do so failed, and she was subsequently beheaded. She was said to have been transported by angels to Mount Sinai, which is why her chapels are found in such dramatic, hilly situations.

On Old May Day in 1993, St Catherine's Chapel was the setting for a celebration of the Swannery's 800th anniversary, when a glorious confusion of old entertainments were brought back to life by the Theatre of the Heart. Among them were giant puppets, Maypole dancers, hobby-horses, stilt walkers, fire-jugglers, and a thirst-quenching cider stall. There was, too, a solitary magpie figure representing that dapper and rapacious bird, bringer of bad tidings, which was ritually buried among the pebbles on the beach below. A wreath of flowers was then tossed from a boat into the sea's rough waves.

Floral sacrifice has long been a custom in Abbotsbury, and is performed on the 13th of May every year. Wreaths of flowers, one for each fishing boat, are cast into the water to propitiate the sea god Neptune, and so ensure a plentiful supply of fish.

The practice still continues in the village, despite the dearth of inshore fishermen, but it no longer survives in other places along Chesil Bank, villages such as Swyre and Puncknowle, where single garlands were once thrown into the sea. In Burton Bradstock, too, garlands (though smaller than those of Abbotsbury) were cast into the waters, a custom which came to an end, like so many others, in 1914. Garland Day in Burton was observed, with more precision, on the 12th of the month, eleven days after the new May Day. The children went round the houses singing the (curiously literary) 'Mayflower Song'.

Beautiful May, so fair, so bright,
Starting forth from wintery night
As to the heavens the lovely stars
So to the earth these flowerets are
Beautiful may, flowery May,
Queen of the seasons, beautiful May.

In a good year Portlanders too celebrated, though more heartily, with hurdy-gurdy, sticky treacle buns and, according to the *Dorset County Chronicle*, 'warbling local performers of the younger branches of families, with older females…'

Meanwhile, in Langton Herring – or so Wilkinson Sherren claimed in 1902 in *The Wessex of Romance* – the villagers took a different approach. 'Before the nets are taken to the beach the contents of a 7lb tin of biscuits are scattered on the adjacent field by the fishermen, in the hope that it will ensure a good season'. Neptune perhaps had a sweet tooth…

An Abbotsbury fisherman, Cyril Toms, recalled his own childhood Garland Days, when he and the other children would go around the village, collecting wild and cultivated flowers from field and garden. Some of the villagers even grew blooms especially for the occasion. All the flowers were then placed in a tin bath of water to keep them fresh until they were needed, when they were mounted on frames of wire and willow boughs. Canon Mayo, observing the ceremony in 1893, said that the garlands were 'as wide as a child's hoop' and were crowned with intercepting arches, which in photographs gives them a top-heavy appearance.

Bearing the garlands, the children went from door to door, and collected pennies from each household. Before the flowers were finally cast into the sea they were displayed on the war memorial in the churchyard, and were blessed.

And what beauty this flower show
carried by child on a willow pole
Buttercups, daisies, flox, sweetpeas,
Done all to cast upon the sea
To thank our Lord for the food he brings
And to herald the start of another new spring.

Cyril Toms, 'The Garland'

*

According to a vague entry in Hutchins, some 'old and very peculiar' fishing customs had existed in Abbotsbury alongside Garland Day, although by the time of the third edition of his history in 1863, they were thought to have died out. Every Monday, before a boat was launched for the week, the Captain would lead his crew in prayers and the fishermen, removing their caps, would fall to their knees and silently request God's 'protection and favour'. However, as these prayers, both on the shore and 'in the flagon-houses' were often succeeded by blasphemy and drunkenness, 'they were very properly laid aside'.

The boat's skipper also decided on the distribution of any profits from the week's catches (unless they were so negligible that they were simply shared out among the ship's crew). Cyril Toms knew all about the sharing out of a disappointingly 'small catch'. The cry went up, 'whose are these?' (pronounced 'oobethese?')

> I, being the lad, would hide behind the blind side of the boat where I could not see what was going on. Then the few fish caught would be put into lots upon the beach, amongst the lots would be a large stone; a hat; a small salmon peel; a pile of pebbles and so on. The skipper, my father [Leonard Toms], would point to three mackerel in a pile shouting 'Oobethese?' and I would shout back "Gunner Eley's!" Gunner would pick up his few mackerel with a "Well done me son". My father would shout again pointing at another lot: "Oobethese?" "Harold Young's!" I would shout out. "Huh, a blooming stone's no good to I!" and with a huff would accept his lot. "Oobethese?" again would be the cry, "the skipper's!" I'd shout. Had

> I done the right thing this time or not? I'd soon find out when it was all over. "You noggle head!" he'd say, "couldn't you have just a little peep, before you shout my name?" Of course I would *never* do such a thing.

A poor catch might be blamed on such bad practices as Sunday fishing, or using fish to manure the land, or setting off on a Monday without the customary prayers. However poor the catch, though, the lord of the manor fared better than most with his payment. As well as receiving an annual rent from each boat, he could lay claim to the 'prize fish' – the finest specimen caught that day from every catch – at a price which remained unchanged from monastic times. If the catch of one lerret was poor or non-existent, while other craft returned laden, then that lerret was thought to be bewitched. The antidote to such a curse was to attach a mackerel stuck with pins to the boat's rudder.

Every Saturday evening the crew would gather at the captain's house where they were offered beer and bread and cheese, and the takings were divided among them. They thanked God for his bounty, but then rather spoilt the effect by adding, 'The God who gave us this can give us more'.

The fishing season was from March to Midsummer. When the mackerel rose, the sea would be dark and heaving with fish. The water was scanned from various vantage points for potential shoals. One of the lookouts was on Punch's Knoll, the wooded hill above the village to which it gave its name. There is a ruined building on the Knoll, which gives a wide-angled view of sea and shore, and was used by revenue officers, smugglers and fishermen alike. In Swyre,

*Mackerel fishing at Abbotsbury (*E V Tanner*).*

they watched by the village cross. At Burton Bradstock, in front of the cliff-top villas, is a decaying promontory which was once another lookout. Here a long horn was used to summon the crews, and the cry went up 'Mackerel! Mackerel! Mackerel!', while at Abbotsbury, the ruins of Strangways Castle provided a further useful vantage point.

Fish dealers (or 'jutes') came to Burton from Merriot in Somerset. They were said to be 'descendents of some sort of Gypsy tribe, and…spoke in a separate language of their own'. The jutes arrived in pony carts and whiled away their waiting time by playing cards on the cliff or drinking cider in the local pubs. Once purchased, the catches were packed into boxes and sent by train to London, Bath and Bristol. This sounds a simple operation, but it wasn't always straightforward. A Langton Herring fisherman called Dick took a boxful of eels to Weymouth to catch the 9.40 evening train to Waterloo. Unfortunately, he failed to secure the lid, and the eels escaped, writhing and sliding over platform and lines. The 9.40 train to London was not on time that night.

When the fishing was good, the beach at Burton Bradstock was so crowded that it was said to resemble 'a country fair'. The women of the village hawked fish themselves, carrying their baskets for miles. Miss Agnes Coombs specialised in shellfish, and old Tom Browne, aided by his crutches and several pints of cider, scratched a living by his sales. A flat-topped wall, known as 'Down Corner', served as the village fish market.

There were the usual fishermen's tales. It was claimed that among the catches was a 'Beaumaris shark' whose capture involved fourteen horses and a host of men. Another shark, a basking one, obligingly yielded 'four hogsheads of oil of excellent quality'. An undated cutting, probably from a contemporary edition of the *Gentleman's Magazine*, tells of a 'monstrous nondescript, justly called the Wonder of the Deep' which was found dead on Abbotsbury beach on May 4th 1801, and was so large that spectators could walk right through it. Two years later the vast creature was exhibited at the Pantheon on London's Oxford Street.

On regular fishing days in Abbotsbury, the knocker-up, a young village lad, would wake the crews at half past three in the morning. Most of the fishermen were part-timers, having different jobs during the day and fishing at night and during the weekends. They would make their way down to the beach, which was a mile and a half from the village. Sometimes the crews included women, Cyril Toms's elder sister among them.

(At Portland, when the men were absent, women were known to take out the boat themselves. In May 1852 a female crew landed two thousand mackerel.)

All along Chesil Bank the mackerel were caught by 'shooting the seine'. The seine was a large net, with a drawstring to close it up at one end and two arms, to which ropes were attached. One rope was coiled up in the lerret, the other, the 'lawn end' was held by a line of the crew up along the beach. In seine fishing, the lerret came into its own, its flat-bottomed design being suited to shallow water, while the double end avoided the need to turn and turn about. The lower edge of the net was weighed down with pebbles, selected from the Portland section of the Bank and drilled with holes. The upper edge of the net was fringed with corks.

Some of the crew took their places in the lerret, those on shore pushed the boat out to sea. The captain jumped aboard, and they were off. Keeping the boat parallel with the shore, they shot the seine, and then those in the lerret would leap out into the water to tug the ship-end rope to the shore, with the help of the incoming tide. Those on the shore would draw in the lawn end at the same time.

The mackerel's green and silver
Sides, its tail so swift will save its
hide.

Cyril Toms

Scooping the fish from the net was known as 'dipping out'. Mackerel are slippery customers and, on examination, the contents of the net as Toms ruefully noted, might yield 'one dozen mackerel, two jelly fish, a large stone, and a lot of seaweed' – or it could contain five hundred stone of gleaming fish. Cyril and his father Leonard would sometimes cook a few of the fresh fish in a bucket heated by a small fire underneath. 'Incidentally one never lit a fire on the beach itself,' Toms wrote, 'because once the pebbles became hot they would explode like hand grenades'.

East of Abbotsbury, the trows used to cross the Fleet and reach the waiting lerrets on the shingle were painted in red and white. They were also used by the Ilchester family for game shooting: each trow being named after a different kind of wild fowl.

Before over-fishing and quotas put an end to the old ways, the sea was alive with fish – not just mackerel and herring, but also sprats in the autumn, whiting and skate. The fishermen went trawling. Further out at sea, herring were fished on winter nights by the light of lanterns. Mackerel are still caught by rod and line, known as 'feathering' because the hooks on the lines were baited with cock feathers. Seine fishing also declined because, like the maintenance of the old water-meadows along the River Frome, the system was highly labour-intensive. In addition, the method was restricted by the need to be inshore, leaving deeper sea shoals out of reach.

*

Eternal Father, strong to save
Whose arm hath bound the restless wave
Who bidd'st the mighty ocean deep
Its own appointed limits keep

Oh, hear us when we cry to Thee
For those in peril on the sea.

Hymn by William Whiting

While some crews ventured out to sea in search of fish, others travelled further still, sailing across the wild expanses of the Atlantic Ocean to Newfoundland, where Englishmen had been fishing since the sixteenth century. In 1610 the adventurers of the London and Bristol Company for the Plantation of Newfoundland – from Dorset and Devon – began to exploit the territory, and by 1674 a Royal Charter had been granted to them, with control being vested in the mayors of West Country ports, including Lyme Regis and Weymouth. The Newfoundland Act of 1697–99 gave the merchants still more authority.

Some of the merchants' servants were sent out to catch, salt, and export the fish, usually returning in the winter. Others decided to settle permanently in Newfoundland, choosing the area where others from their home port were fishing. These 'planters' traded with the merchants, and while the latter regarded Newfoundland as 'a great ship moored to England', the planters were anxious to secure 'peace, justice and security' for themselves during the long dark winters. Their wishes were eventually granted. In 1793, a Supreme Court of Justice was established, and the Dorset mayors had to 'take cognisance' of all offences committed on the soil of Newfoundland. In 1816 the first resident governor was appointed.

Throughout the eighteenth century the Newfoundland fishery was the source of most of Dorset's maritime trade, and of the capital investment of the county's ports (Poole being the most prominent). Its peak was during the Napoleonic Wars. Salted cod and its oil made up the chief imports from Newfoundland, along with furs and skins, seal-oil and salmon and timber. Smaller and less perfect fish – 'refuse' – were sent to the West Indies as food for the unfortunate slaves.

The boats also carried passengers – the adventurous, the ambitious and the desperate – in search of seasonal labour, not all of whom made any profit from their journeying. Life in Newfoundland, as some of the folk songs told, could be even harder than the lives they had left behind them.

Come all ye good people,
I'll sing you a song,
About the poor people,
How they get along.
They'll start in the Spring,
Finish up in the Fall,
And when it's all over
They have nothing at all.
And it's hard, hard times.

As well as the prospective hopeful workers, the boats carried clothes and shoes for the settlers. Cabbages grown in West Bay gardens, at the end of the Southover allotments in Burton Bradstock, were wrapped in damp sackcloth and exported as greenstuff to feed the fishermen. By the 1780s the cargoes included the rope, twine, nets and sailcloth which were then being produced in the Dorset villages.

When the fishing ceased, Bridport continued to send these products to Newfoundland.

Further evidence of the extent and importance of the trade in the county comes from an unexpected quarter. Douglas Northover, a man from an old West Dorset family of fishermen, farmers and net braiders, compiled the *Language of Old Burton, Burton Bradstock, Dorset* after the Second World War. It is a heady mixture of the local, the vernacular and the downright peculiar, providing a (somewhat quaint) picture of life in the village. Some of the expressions can also be found in William Barnes's *Glossary,* words like *dumble dore* for 'bumble bee', *nestle-tripe* for the 'smallest pig in the litter', *yop,* meaning 'to gossip' and *barken*, a 'cow barton'. Many others words are absent from it. Barnes's glossary was chiefly concerned with farming terms: with the woods and fields of home. For some reason he turned his back on the sea, both in his lexicographical works and in his dialect poetry. He also shied away from unpleasantness: for instance, although he included the unsavoury *mixen* meaning 'midden' in the glossary, he avoided any definition of the word. Barnes would not have dreamt of including Northover's *turd bird*, a skua (a bird which 'eats fish that it forces other birds to disgorge') or *madder,* meaning 'the pus from a septic wound'.

Northover has some suspiciously literary entries, such as the florid 'Mayflower Song' for Garland Day (which is quoted above). Like some of the Edwardian folksong collectors, he perhaps could not resist the occasional embellishment of his material, while a number of his entries could comfortably find space in that classic parody of rustic life, *Cold Comfort Farm*. A *nuddick* is a small hill, *Panshards* are defined as 'broken crockery or glass', and *Panshard's Night* is Halloween, which has inspired the following ditty

It's Panshard night tonight!
It's Panshard Night tonight!
Adam and Eve and Pinch-me-tight
It's Panshard Night tonight!

More modern-sounding entries include the endearing *Monkey's birthday,* which is said to mean 'rain and sunshine at the same time', and *Tidderfer la*, which, we are told, means 'fancy dress'.

But the bulk of the entries concern the sea and fishing, and have the confident precision of close experience. Like the language of the stonemasons on Portland, technical terms are more likely to survive than other dialect words, especially if the practices they describe are still current. *Calling the fresh* was the task of a young boy, who would run through the village with a string of mackerel, shouting out the news of the first mackerel catch of the day. *Glate* was 'an oily patch of sea usually denoting the presence of herring or pilchards'. A *queer man* was an illegal catch, such as salmon or game. A *skewer* was 'a wave rolling along the shore, making it difficult to launch a boat'. And seagulls circling the sea in search of food were said to be 'towering'.

In an article in *Lore and Language* in 1989, Martin J Lovelace reproduced Northover's wordlist, noting any dialect terms which could also be found in the *Dictionary of Newfoundland English,* published in 1982. These included *The Barber,* which was defined as 'a land mist drifting out to sea on frosty nights, when frost settled on boat and clothing'. *May water*, meanwhile, was defined as dirty water in the spring sea. Such water is 'devoid of plankton, therefore [there are] no fish'. *Zun dogs* are 'sheets of light in the sky, believed to foretell bad weather' – known as *sun hounds* in Newfoundland.

Lovelace found even more parallels when it came to terms relating to seine fishing, which was practised in both countries. *Linnets*, for example, were 'folds in the arms or sweeps of a seine, pulled out when [the] net is coming ashore to drive fish into bunt'. A *prior cork* was 'a small buoy attached to the centre of a seine to show where the bunt (bag) is when fishing'.

In Dorset, such dialect words for aspects of the complexities of seine-fishing were not, of course, restricted to Burton Bradstock. They would have been heard in Abbotsbury and Langton and all along the Chesil Bank, as well as being echoed in distant Newfoundland. (Some of the surnames the villages shared also made the journey and survive today, reminders of a joint maritime history.)

In spite of the shared language, fishing was a competitive business along the Chesil. The drystone wall running down through the cattle-trodden, clayey fields to Burton Mere – known as the 'third wall' – provided an unofficial boundary observed by the Burton and Bexington fishermen. In Burton Bradstock itself, unrhythmical rowing by crews was known sarcastically as the 'Portland stroke'. The fishermen were as proud of their own territories as Sir John Strangways had been of his estates during the English Civil War.

Troubled Waters

The sea is calm to-night,
The tide is full, the moon lies fair
Upon the Straits; – on the French coast the light
Gleams and is gone; the cliffs of England stand,
Glimmering and vast, out in the tranquil bay.
Come to the window, sweet is the night-air!
Only, from the long line of spray
Where the ebb meets the moon-blanch'd land,
Listen! You hear the grating roar
Of pebbles which the waves suck back, and fling,
At their return, up the high strand,
Begin, and cease, and then again begin,
With tremulous cadence slow, and bring
The eternal note of sadness in.

Matthew Arnold, 'Dover Beach'

THE MANOR HOUSE IN PUNCKNOWLE is shielded by the parish church. Perhaps because of this position, the manor's east front (as Nikolaus Pevsner noted) is 'endearingly round-shouldered' and relaxed. But the gardens display a stiff parade of pleached limes, providing a suitably martial setting for the house's most famous occupant, Major-General Henry Needham Scope Shrapnel (1761–1847), officer and inventor.

One of Shrapnel's visitors in Puncknowle was William Barnes, who in his younger years worked as a schoolmaster. He taught many subjects, for which – after discovering the dullness of existing texts – he wrote his own child-friendly and informative school books. One of his favourite subjects was mathematics, a subject not then held in high esteem, being regarded as 'fit only for mechanics and engineers', which was a state of affairs he hoped to alter. Barnes's first mathematical pamphlet, published in 1832, is now lost, though copies of his second, 'A Few Words on the Advantages of a More Common Adoption of the Mathematics as a Branch of Education or Subject of Study' still survive. The pamphlet's dedication is 'To Major-General Shrapnel, the greatest mathematician to whom the author has had the honor of being introduced, and to whose kindness much of his own proficiency in the exact sciences must be attributed, he most respectfully and gratefully dedicates the following essay.'

How Barnes was first introduced to Shrapnel is not known, but he seemed to regard him as his mathematical mentor, despite the fact that the Major-General had used these studies in his invention in 1784 of a particularly nasty weapon of war, to which he gave his name. Barnes used to joke that he had helped with the invention – although he wasn't born at the time – and it is surprising that such a gentle and kindly man should wish to be associated with a lethal cannon ball which, when fired, shot to pieces in mid-air, aiming to do as much harm as possible to enemy personnel. (Although Shrapnel was promoted for his work, even some of his fellow-officers found the invention 'unsporting'.)

Beyond Shrapnel's manor house, Puncknowle village merges into Swyre, which had its own combative monuments. The inn sits high on the coast road, commanded from the roof by a rampant red bull which gives the pub its name. This beast was formerly flanked by a pair of old sea mines, souvenirs of war from Lyme Bay.

In the silent waters of the lagoon below, another now-famous weapon of war underwent some of its initial tests. The 'Bouncing Bomb' was tried out three times during December 1942, using a bomber flown from Dorset's airfield at nearby RAF Warmwell. Each time, the bomb failed to bounce. According to Iris Burgin, a resident of Langton Herring for fifty-one years, who was then living in one of the coastguard cottages there, the test area lay between Moonfleet Manor and New Barn Farm, Rodden. Iris Burgin was thus well-placed to witness the progress of the experiment. Scientific instruments and a camera were set up on top of the rainwater reservoir in front of her house in order to monitor the flights. Years later, she wrote about the experience of seeing one of the much more successful tests of 1943.

> Watching with my family the Peaches from an upper window about 2 pm we heard a plane approaching. This had a large white ball suspended underneath. It made a dummy run from Moonfleet House to New Barn over the waters of the Fleet. On the second run it released the ball which bounced on the water westwards. It floated for a few minutes then sank in the mud. The plane

> circled again and another ball was dropped successfully. The assembled team seemed very pleased. The balls were not recovered.

The bombs used in the second run, though, were afterwards recovered. A wooden landing stage was built at Langton Hive for this purpose. Experiments then continued in other parts of the country, after local complaints that the testing was disturbing the Abbotsbury swans during their mating and nest-making season.

The bomb's creator was an engineer named Barnes Wallis (1887–1979) who became assistant chief designer in the aviation section of Vickers-Armstrong. As a child he had holidayed in Dorset, and knew the terrain. After the outbreak of war in 1939 he wrote a paper called 'A Note on a Method of Attacking the Axis Powers', which argued that paralysis of the enemy's power supplies would prevent them from continuing to fight. His intention was to destroy German reservoir dams. His bomb, which actually ricocheted rather than bounced, was designed to skim across the water until it reached its target, where it would sink and explode against the dam wall. (When developing the bomb, Wallis rehearsed by skimming stones across the surface of a water tank.)

His design worked. On May 16th– 17th 1943, nineteen aircraft, with a total crew of 133 men of the 617 Squadron, attacked the Mohne, Sorpe and Eder dams in Germany. Their mission was to create a shortage of water in the Ruhr industrial region, and they were able to use Lancaster bombers, rather than the earlier heavier planes, thanks to the streamlining of the bomb's design during the experiments in the Fleet. Bill Bryson, in *The Road to Little Dribbling*, has his own disillusioned interpretation of the outcome.

> In practice, the scheme didn't really work. The low-flying planes were easy targets for German gunners – 40 per cent of the squadron didn't return from the first mission – and many bombs exploded harmlessly in the water or bounced straight over the dam walls and detonated in neighbouring fields. Only one dam was seriously breached; the floodwaters from it killed about 1,700 people, but those were mostly Allied prisoners, so that in fact Barnes Wallis killed more people on his own side than on the German one.

This however seems to be an minority verdict, and one which disregards the courage of the pilots, and the boldness of the operation. The film of *The Dambusters* – which was released in 1955, and continues to be screened – paints a patriotic picture of the undoubtedly daring raids, seeing them as successful, though not without regard for the human cost, which included the deaths of several hundred Russian prisoners of war.

One of the test bombs, dropped in March 1943 – a massive and quaintly dimpled pudding – is on display in the Swannery gardens. Like much of the British coast, Lyme Bay's shores are studded with the redundant relics of war: pillboxes, stumps of brick and pebbles trapped in concrete, warped remnants of old defences, dating mostly from the 1940s. Many of those found in the Fleet have been adopted as

Abbotsbury's Bouncing Bomb (Mick Orr)

shelters by fishermen. Tank traps, which are poetically known as 'dragons' teeth', still lurk on the Abbotsbury beach.

During the Second World War, one plane was shot down in the Fleet. It lay helplessly in the lagoon's thick mud which preserved the machine so well that, when it was eventually retrieved, it looked as bright as new. On the Fleet's shore below Moonfleet Manor, amongst the odds and ends of seashells, pebbles and eel grass, spent cartridges can still be dug out of the sand.

Fear of invasion has often troubled Dorset, vulnerable as the county is to incursions from the French coast. For centuries a simple but effective device, the beacon, was used to warn of any potential threats. The word is of Saxon origin, but it's thought that fire-beacons did not start to be used until the fourteenth century. It is known that when a

French invasion was expected in 1539, the beacons were lit accordingly. A map of 1593 shows seventeen coastal beacon sites in Dorset, and there were probably a further seventeen inland. Along the Chesil, beacons could be found near Wyke Church, at Abbotsbury Castle, on Beacon Knap in Swyre, at Puncknowle and on North Hill, Burton Bradstock. In her *Dorset Elizabethans*, Rachel Lloyd describes the beacons as 'cones surmounted by brushwood, with ladders running up their sides, and up them men could go to light the warning flames at their crest'. They were lit in sequence, one after another, until the coastline was illuminated by a line of fire. In 1897 on Tennyson Down, Isle of Wight, a beacon was removed after the poet's death and a memorial cross erected in its place. The stump of the old beacon has been moved to the edge of a track below, and a modern half-size replica placed beside it.

There had been other, more spectral, warnings of danger, such as the one which is mentioned in Holinshed's *Chronicles*, quoted by Hutchins in his history.

> In November 1457, in Portland, was seen a cock coming out of the sea, having a great crest on his head, a great red beard, and legs half a yard long. He stood on the water and crowed three times, and every time turned himself about, and beckoned with his head north, south, and west. He was in colour like a pheasant, and when he had crowed he vanished.

Rumours of further fanciful sightings circulated in 1804–05, when fear of French invasion during the Napoleonic

Wars was at its panicky height. Intricate plans were drawn up for the defence of the realm. A sturdy marbled notebook, belonging to an unknown Dorset clerk, provides a detailed record of some of these plans, listing officers, available weapons and schemes for the distribution of local forces. Included too, is an inventory of all the livestock. (This latter must have been a thankless task, and one which was unlikely to be accurate.) As for the beacons, the notebook stipulates that, on the lighting of any coastal beacon, the 'companies under arms' were to assemble promptly, while the firing of inland beacons should act 'as a caution to prepare them to be in readiness'. Although in the end Napoleon never attempted a landing, the county was nervously alert for such a disaster.

More than two hundred years beforehand, the county had also been ready for the advent of 'the most happy fleet' – the *Felissima Armada* – which formed perhaps the greatest threat the country ever faced until the outbreak of the Second World War. The attack on Elizabethan England was mounted by Philip II of Spain, the most powerful man in the world, in July 1588. He sent 125 ships, tightly packed with thirty thousand sailors and soldiers, horses and heavy guns, galley slaves and gentlemen adventurers. They were accompanied by monks, whose purpose was to provide pastoral care for the fleet and, it was planned, to reconvert the Protestant English to Catholicism. Thus the mission had a double purpose: conversion of the heretics, and the curbing of their impudent incursions into the New World of the Americas, a territory which Philip considered his own.

Over the previous hundred years, the New World ventures which so enraged Philip had toughened England's sailors. The country was becoming a maritime nation. It's generally thought that by the time of the Armada the English had developed lighter and faster vessels than the Spaniards, with better navigational instruments and skills – and they were aware that an invasion was impending. Mariners, even in the small coastal villages of Dorset, such as Swyre, Langton Herring and Chickerell, were being commandeered along with their ships.

In 1585 there was a survey of the Dorset coast, to identify the places where the enemy might try to land, prior to launching an invasion. Portland Roads, Weymouth and Melcombe Regis all had expanses of deep water which were out of the reach of the defending cannons positioned at Sandsfoot and Portland Castles in Weymouth Bay. (It was suspected that a stretch of a mile and a half along the Chesil near Wyke Regis might be another possible landing-point for the enemy troops.)

The long-awaited fleet finally arrived on July 20 1588. (The dates given in this account are those of the Julian calendar which was still in use in England. By then the Spanish were using the Gregorian version.) In the words of Rachel Lloyd: 'Captain Fleming of the *Golden Hind* saw, by the light of the moon, a great black crescent moving slowly off the Lizard. An unexpected shape resembling that of a bat – the Armada.' Immediately, the beacons were lit. The fleet must have been a terrifying sight, a dark and towering mass, in a crescent seven miles wide. The ships kept sharply and precisely together as they sailed along the Channel. Unknown to the English, the naval commander of the Spanish fleet, the Duke of Medina Sidonia, had been instructed not to engage with the enemy unless absolutely necessary, but to wait until the Spanish army, under the Duke of Parma, had reached England and joined forces with them.

The first battle, off the Eddystone at Plymouth on July 21, was indecisive, though differences in the tactics of the two fleets immediately emerged, as Lloyd describes:

> Never had the Spaniards seen such rapid fire at sea; the English ships were small and nimbler and their method of fighting a new one, for they poured in a broadside, then passed on, came about and poured in another. The Spanish were unable to grapple and board the English, the traditional way of fighting at sea, indeed with their great ships with the high towers they could fight no other way. They were unable, during all the fighting of the next few days, ever to board the enemy.

Two Spanish ships were accidental casualties of this encounter. One was the *Rosario*, which was damaged when she collided with another Spanish vessel, and had to be taken in tow among the Armada's ships. The other was the *San Salvador*, which was discovered by the Lord High Admiral, Charles Howard of Effingham, abandoned in Lyme Bay after a gunpowder explosion on her upper deck. She was taken into Weymouth, and stripped of her remaining ammunition, while eight 'badly burned' survivors were rescued. The *Rosario* fell behind the fleet when her ropes failed, and was sneakily captured under cover of darkness by squadron commander Sir Francis Drake, in his ship the

Revenge. This action was against Admiral Howard's orders, but Drake, pirate that he was, knew that he would have equal rights with Queen Elizabeth to claim the prize money for the capture. This did not endear him to his fellow-sailors.

Howard's main aim was to keep the Spanish fleet offshore, to prevent them at all costs from landing on the English coast. On Tuesday July 23, the Armada approached Portland Bill ahead of the English, and with the wind veering easterly in its favour. Fearing that they might try to enter Weymouth Bay, Howard turned his fleet about. He was apparently hoping that the ships of the Armada would follow – and most of them obligingly did so.

However, the largest ship in either fleet, the *Triumph*, whose captain (and the commander of the fourth squadron) was Martin Frobisher, remained under Portland Bill accompanied by five armed merchantmen. Frobisher was something of a maverick. A pirate and explorer, who had made three trips to the New World in search of gold (which turned out to be of the fool's variety), he was also quick to wrath, and as slippery as the eels on the bed of the Fleet. When four of the Armada's galleasses – swift ships with a crew of 300 soldiers and sailors, plus 300 rowers – approached them, Frobisher fired the *Triumph*'s guns into the rowing decks, doubly disabling oars and men. Howard, with seven other ships, sailed to the rescue, driving the Spanish vessels away.

Reports of this battle long ago are clumsily conflicting and shamelessly patriotic, but it seems possible that Frobisher was either attempting to lure the Spanish ships to their destruction on the Portland Race or the sandbanks of the Shambles, waters he knew well – or that he was preventing the Armada's fleet from landing in Portland Harbour. He might also have been making a retaliatory gesture towards his rival, Drake, with an unorthodox action of his own.

Medina Sidonia never did attempt to land during his voyage up the Channel, and the end came on July 29 at the Battle of Gravelines, off the northern coast of France. The Spanish fleet had dropped anchor, and were waiting to be joined by the Duke of Parma's army, which was being blockaded in the harbour by Dutch flyboats which controlled that area. The Armada managed to escape up the east coast of England, harried by their enemy. The order was issued to return to Spain, but the weather was against them, and many ships came to grief off the shores of Scotland and Ireland.

In 1592, to commemorate the defeat of the Spanish Armada, Howard commissioned (and paid for) a series of ten tapestries, depicting richly-embroidered scenes from significant battles – including the clash off the Isle of Portland (portrayed with a background of oddly rounded hillocks). The tapestries were huge, about 14 feet high and 28 feet wide, and originally decorated the walls of the Admiral's evidently large Chelsea home.

In 1644 they were transferred to the House of Lords where, most presciently, the designer John Pine, aware of their importance, made engravings from them. The engravings were published in 1739. During the huge fire in 1834 which devastated most of the old Palace of Westminster, the tapestries went up in flames and were completely destroyed. Shortly before his death in 1861 Prince Albert was planning to make copies from Pine's engravings, but it was not until 2010 that the replacement paintings were finally installed in the Prince's Chamber. Thanks to a private donation they, like the originals, had cost the country nothing.

Once presented as a glorious victory for the English, to the twenty-first century landlubber the battles appear slow and blundering, with the weather as the deciding factor – though it's intriguing to imagine the massive fleet sailing threateningly along the lonely Chesil Bank. Centuries after the Armada, though, Lyme Bay was to play a more important part in a much wider war.

*

An image of the Egyptian-yellow cliffs between West Bay and Burton Bradstock served as a logo for the television crime drama *Broadchurch*, for which West Bay provided a prime location. These sandstone cliffs are unstable and often troubled by rock falls which can be abrupt and lethal.

In 1944, a Burton Bradstock girl called Janet Guppy was, as usual, walking along the East Cliff on her way to school, when she thought she heard some unrecognisable sounds. The cliffs were enclosed by bristling barbed wire, but she was able to peer over to see soldiers scrambling up the defensive line of cliffs, with debris flying around them. A rare film clip of that year shows a swarm of men clambering up the Burton rock face, on flimsy, swaying rope ladders.

These soldiers were not German invaders, as might have been feared, but American Rangers, troops of the 1st and 29th Divisions of the US Army. The cliffs of Burton Bradstock had been carefully selected for their mission, as they were the mirror images of the cliffs at Pointe du Hoc on the Normandy coast, matching them in height and geological composition.

The soldiers were preparing for D-Day, the day of the Allies' attack on occupied France.

Lyme Bay had been an area of strategic importance from the start of the Second World War. It was at the centre of an area targeted by Hitler for invasion in 1940, and became part of a major line of defence, with Burton Bradstock as one of its training grounds. American soldiers were training along the south coast: the Castletown D-Day Centre on the Isle of Portland tells the history of the many American troops stationed there.

The first plan in 1940 had been for a raid on Dieppe, and was a failure. Troops were misdirected, or never even arrived on French soil. In 1942 a second, combined operations assault fared little better, and it became clear that the Allies were not yet ready for a full-blown attack.

American forces sailed to join the Canadians and British forces gathering on the coast. In Burton Bradstock they were billeted to the east and west of the village, with some of them based in the Freshwater holiday camp. (As segregation was still being enforced in America, any black GIs would have been billeted separately.) The British people were generally regarded by the GIs as stiff and standoffish and so, since the villagers were not allowed to enter the camps, a young girl called Betty (Liz) Mackay, an evacuee from London, was chosen as the face of the English welcome. This may not have been necessary, as the many contemporary photographs show the friendships which easily grew up between troops and villagers. Most of the inhabitants had not seen an American before (and certainly not a black one). They seemed glamorous figures, dispensers of chocolate and hair ribbons. In return for the gifts, the villagers offered the soldiers hospitality. They took the GIs rabbiting, and invited them to Sunday lunch. Soldiers are seen refuelling their jeep at the village petrol pumps while indifferent cows lumber past along the street. The village women began to braid nets for camouflage, rather than for catching fish. Troops at Freshwater are shown having their hair cut on the beach.

The long-planned-for D-Day came on June 6 1944, by which time there were 89,000 British, Canadian and American forces in waiting along the south coast. Janet Guppy was a witness to the departure of the Burton Bradstock contingent of troops. The sea, she said, was 'black with boats'. 'Operation Neptune' was successful and proved to be the beginning of the end of the war – but it came at a heavy cost. Half of the soldiers who left Burton Bradstock that morning were killed or injured on the very same day. The village must have suddenly become a silent, empty place, especially after the terrible news of the casualties filtered back.

Few traces remain of the soldiers' visit, apart from the stories and local reminiscences. A pillbox squats awkwardly on Bind Barrow above the Hive, and two of the village's tank traps were recycled by local farmers, to be used as lowly milk stands.

*

At the Wyke Regis end of the causeway, by Ferry Bridge, the newly-built Port Authority Sanitary Hospital was soon to become less isolated. Its new neighbour was the Whitehead Torpedo Works, which were established in 1891, eleven years after the Hospital's own foundation. They were an ill-assorted pairing of cure and kill.

The first self-propelled torpedo was created in 1868, by the inventor and engineer Robert Whitehead (1823–1905) and remained for a while the prime weapon of destruction employed in sea warfare. It was a versatile weapon, which could be fired from underwater by submarines, or from the decks of destroyers, or else dropped from aircraft.

Whitehead was then chief engineer (and power behind the throne) at the Fiume factory in what is now Croatia, which designed and built warships for the Austro-Hungarian Empire. On the recommendation of another torpedo expert, Edwin Payne Gellway, the Royal Navy placed an order with the factory. When concerns were expressed about importing such a significant weapon, Whitehead decided to set up a torpedo works back in England, and a suitable site was found at Wyke Regis.

The foundation stone for the factory was laid on April 11 1891. The eight-acre site lay between the causeway road and the railway line to Portland. In 1909, a new station, called Wyke Regis Halt – despite the fact it was some distance from the old village – was opened to serve the factory. Under the railway was a jetty which stretched for over one thousand yards out into the harbour, complete with a narrow gauge railway line. This carried the torpedoes to waiting boats, from which they were tested. (The supports for the pier are still visible at low tide.)

To accommodate the influx of workers, a 'New Wyke' began to be developed, formed mainly of brick terraces. These included Ferry Bridge Cottages, a triangular group of houses, with a central green which served as a drying-area for the nets used to fish the torpedoes out after their testing. Methodist churches, a school, the Wyke Hotel (now the Wyke Smugglers pub) and the Working Men's Club were other buildings of a similar period, built for the same purpose.

When Robert Whitehead died in 1905 he was succeeded by Captain Gallwey, who lived at 'The Beacon', 91 Wyke Regis Road, so-called because it was close to the site of the old Wyke beacon. The house was demolished in 1936, but Gallwey is remembered in the name of a nearby road.

Unfortunately, the Captain died only a year after his predecessor, and no one could be found to replace him. The Admiralty was anxious not to let the business fall into foreign hands, and so approached two companies, Armstrong-Whitworth and Vickers Ltd who became major

At the Torpedo Works c.1912.

shareholders, while the Whitehead family continued to hold just under 50%. (One of Armstrong's directors, John Meade Falkner, held ten shares.)

In 1914 the Admiralty took charge of the factory for the duration of the war. Control afterwards returned briefly to Armstrong-Vickers, but there was little demand for torpedoes by that time, and in 1921 the factory went briefly into liquidation until in 1923 Vickers-Armstrong re-purchased the site as a new company. As the thirties progressed, so did demand for torpedoes, and the Works became a major employer in the district. After the outbreak of the Second World War many of the men were called up, and so the company was obliged to recruit large numbers of women to replace them.

Close as they were to Portland Harbour and its ships, the Works were an easy target for German aircraft. They were bombed several times without any major damage – except to their own future as, for safety, production was transferred to Bournemouth, Street and Staines. While the war continued however, production at Wyke began to grow. Ferry Bridge, the only road link to Portland, became a centre of activity in 1944, during the preparations for the invasion of Europe, and the waiting American troops found themselves billeted in the long-deserted wards of the old Sanitary Hospital.

After the war, the Works went through different hands. The last torpedo was produced in 1969, and the factory diversified, making a variety of objects, including ice-cream machines, soap stamps, knitting machines and guillotines. The inevitable closure came in 1993, and the site is now occupied by housing. A rather battered foundation stone (for which a search had to be made during demolition in 1997) is displayed among the houses, together with a shiny marble plaque, headed by a fish-like torpedo, which commemorates the recent Harbour Point development.

Whitehead had one more claim to fame, and that was, unexpectedly, a musical one. In 1908, the Austro-Hungarian Navy had assigned Kapitänleutnant Georg Ritter von Trapp to the Fiume factory. While working there, von Trapp met and married Agatha, daughter of Whitehead's son John. Agatha died of diphtheria in 1922, leaving Georg alone with his five motherless children. He employed a governess called Maria to look after his children, and as one of their lessons she taught them how to sing. Later Georg and Maria were married, and had yet more children. They also had some remarkable wartime experiences. Maria von Trapp wrote a book about the family's life, on which yet another famous film – *The Sound of Music* – was based.

However, it emerged that not everyone living along the Chesil Bank was quite as concerned with the protection of their country as the people of this chapter.

The Elm Tree

Chesil Bank is on the move. Year by year it is shifting, irreversibly, imperceptibly, a little closer to the land. Eventually the Fleet lagoon will be completely swallowed up. This slow and furtive action makes the Beach ever more secret, providing cover for the dubious activities of smugglers, wreckers, poachers, pirates – and, notoriously, spies.

The most hidden of the villages along the Fleet is Langton Herring. Well away from the shore, it is also invisible from the coast road entrance, concealed by a grove of trees. Among the trees and brambles hides the medieval Langton Cross, carved in fine, lichened limestone. The Cross is said to celebrate the coming of each New Year by walking through the village and down to the lagoon, to dip its arms into the brackish water.

The Cross would be better having a drink at the pub instead. The elm tree which gave the building its name has died and cannot be replaced, but the inn itself is still thriving, and has been in Langton, 'the long town', for perhaps four hundred years. It was useful as a smuggling haunt, and is rumoured to be riddled with underground tunnels. Ghostly presences were summoned up to scare away the snoopers. There's also a story that in 1780, when a fisherman who was drinking in the pub began to boast excessively about the size of his catch, he was caught out in his lies, chased through the village, captured, and hanged from a heavy beam.

In the later 1950s two regular drinkers at the Elm Tree were a couple from Portland, Harry Houghton and Ethel Gee. Both worked at what was then the major employer on the island: the Underwater Detection Establishment, the UDE (known since 1957 as the Admiralty Underwater Weapons Establishment), which was the centre for NATO's submarine research.

Before she met Harry, Ethel Elizabeth Gee had led a very strait-laced sort of life. Privately educated, she lived with her mother, Lily, her aunt Bessie and uncle Jack – an elderly trio – at 23 Hambro Road, a redbrick terraced house in hilly Fortuneswell. Neighbours remembered 'Bunty', as she was known, enjoying family sing-songs around the piano, stitching away at petit point and enjoying badminton at the local club. She joined the UDE in 1950 as a very minor civil servant in the Stores, but rose to become one of three clerical officers in charge of the drawing office records and of the secret reports on submarine tests at the establishment. The aim of the project was to design and build the first transistorised sonar equipment for the new Dreadnought class of submarine due to be launched in 1963.

She met Harry Houghton in1952 during the course of her work. Eleven years her senior, Houghton was a married man with an adult step-daughter. He had joined the Navy at the age of sixteen, the beginning of a highly-coloured career. After training, he was sent to the China Station, where he spent much of his time smuggling opium or, as he put it, 'dabbling in a few rackets like everyone else'. In their book *Spy Ring*, published in 1961, John Bulloch and Henry Miller, both respected *Daily Telegraph* correspondents, remark that he was already showing his two major character faults, which were 'avarice, and the inability to distinguish between what was permissible and what was completely and morally wrong'. During the Second World War, however, he acquitted himself honourably in various naval actions, and emerged as a full Master-at-Arms: the highest non-commissioned rank in the Royal Navy.

In 1951 he was sent as Naval Attaché's clerk to the British Embassy in Warsaw. He took to the life, and to the Polish vodka, and was often drunk – though not when at work. His marriage was deteriorating, and after his wife accused him of deliberately breaking her leg, he was sent back to England. His sins were regarded as social ones: the reason given for his return was that his post was being downgraded and had become (Houghton claimed) only suitable for a single woman. According to Houghton, too, his wife returned home while he stayed on in Poland, where he had an affair with a Russian woman known as Kartzia, an affair which ultimately led to his downfall.

During his stay in Poland, Houghton's activities were watched by the Russians, who suspected that, as he was such a heavy drinker, he would not be scrupulous about how he earned the money to fund his habit. Back in England he was blackmailed by them into espionage (or so he said). He was told that Kartzia's life would be in danger if he did not agree to co-operate. Greedy for money, he was not difficult to persuade, especially as he was drawn only gradually (but irreversibly) into the network. The Russians were behind the West in their development of submarines, and Houghton was in a position to supply them with information which would help them to catch up. As he appeared to have no blot on his record, he had now been given confidential work at the UDE. The first pieces of information Houghton was asked to supply were in the form of news-cuttings and other such openly available, harmless-seeming, material. He was given a camera shaped like a cigarette lighter for use in photographing objects. Later he was given a second camera, an Exacta, for photographing documents.

He and his wife settled in a semi-detached house outside Weymouth, at 8 Meadow View Road, Broadwey, which was then isolated on the edge of the downs. By 1954 Houghton and Ethel Gee had begun going out together in the evenings. This was probably the last straw for Houghton's wife Peggy. In 1955, sickened by his violence and the financial insecurity caused by his drinking, she separated from her husband. With Ethel's money, Houghton bought a caravan on Portland, in the grounds of Pennsylvania Castle on the cliffs at Church Ope, handy for Ethel's house and for their place of work. He gave Ethel a lift to work every morning and took her back home in the evenings. All of this, on a small island, must have made them both very conspicuous – although they seem to have managed to deceive Ethel's family about their relationship, even when it became a full-blown affair. (On weekend trips to London, they pretended to be staying with imaginary friends called Sue and Bill.)

The caravan on the cliff proved invaluable for the couple. It was somewhere they could meet unobserved and a place where Harry could photograph documents in secret, borrowing them from work on the Saturday, and returning them on the Monday.

By now, Houghton had been moved to the Port Authority Repair Unit in the dockyard. Discovering his bulging wallet, his wife had previously reported him to the Castletown authorities. Her suspicions were made light of, thought to be caused by jealousy of Ethel Gee, but – in case they did have any substance – Harry was transferred. Ironically this move left him in charge of more sensitive material than he had previously handled.

Ignoring her husband's resistance (which Houghton later denied) Peggy began divorce proceedings and was soon to remarry, while Harry moved back to the Meadow View Road house, spending lavish amounts of money on such improvements as new carpets, wall-panelling and a state-of-the-art gramophone. This did not go unnoticed. Where was the money coming from?

Harry Houghton's own account of events, written after his release from prison in 1971, suggests that most of the money came from his black market dealings while he was in Poland. He had imported luxury goods, such as liquor, tobacco and fur coats from England, which he resold at exorbitant prices in Warsaw.

Or so Houghton claimed; the accounts are contradictory. At least four books were published shortly after his trial in 1961, including *Spy Ring*, whose authors had attended the proceedings. The master spy in the Portland ring, Gordon

Arthur Lonsdale, wrote his own memoir *Spy* (claimed to be the first autobiography of its kind) after release from prison in 1965. He complained about the inaccuracy of the previously-published books. Bulloch's and Miller's, he remarked, contained 'distressingly many' errors, due to the unseemly haste with which it was produced. Worse by far though, to his mind, was Comer Clarke's *The War Within*, which had 'howlers' on every page.

Houghton's contribution to the genre, *Operation Portland*, unsurprisingly differs wildly from Lonsdale's account. As Ludovic Kennedy pointed out in his *Portland Spy Case*, 'the detailed truth…is impossible to obtain… because the numerous accounts of it, including those by two of its principal participants (both of them proven liars), contradict each other at numerous turns'. Kennedy's solution to this problem was to write a fictionalised account 'based on [the author's] imagination and all the available evidence, of what he thinks most likely happened', thereby adding another dimension to the tale. (As if the facts weren't enough, Lonsdale added to the mix by implicating James Bond in his memoir.)

Lonsdale consistently lied about his name. It was not Gordon Arnold Lonsdale, as he persisted in saying, but (it was belatedly discovered) Konon Trofimovich Molody, or possibly Georgei Lonov. He also posed as an American Commander called Alec Johnson – he could speak several languages, including English, fluently. Some of them were acquired, like his spying skills, during wartime resistance work in Europe.

In 1945 he married 'a beautiful Polish girl named Halina Panfilowska', a survivor of the labour camps. She 'remained a source of great happiness' to him, although as she was in Russia he seldom saw her, or their children. As a spy, Lonsdale was a true professional, convinced of the rightness of the Communist cause. After the War he hunted Nazis in America until 1955 when, as his 'true self' Gordon Lonsdale he was transferred to Britain. His primary task was to report on the development of biological weapons at Porton Down and activities at the Polaris submarine base in Holy Loch. His Portland work was, he declared, a sideshow: 'In my field… there is abundant evidence that Britain can no longer keep up with the Joneses'. He rather despised Harry, finding him 'vain as well as shifty' and easy to flatter. For his part, Harry claimed to like Lonsdale, while remarking that the Russian 'hardly knew the sharp end of the ship from the blunt end… All he did was pass things on'.

While in Britain, Lonsdale lived for most of the time in the cramped luxury of the White House, an apartment block overlooking Regent's Park, where his neighbours kept themselves to themselves. He was an importer of juke boxes, and became a partner in two vending machine businesses, dispensing chewing gum and bubble gum. Meanwhile, he was passing information on to a couple called the Krogers (not of course their real name, which was Cohen).

Peter and Helen Kroger lived in immaculate respectability in a bungalow at 45 Cranley Drive, Ruislip. Peter Kroger worked as an antiquarian bookseller. His house was full of books and he had a London shop at 190 The Strand. This was more than just a cover for his spying work; he was a respected dealer and a member of the Antiquarian Booksellers Association. His wife was an amateur photographer, though from all accounts she was (like Harry) not a very good one. Both were Communists, and as spies in America had been associated with Julius and Ethel Rosenberg, the couple who were executed for their espionage activities. Peter Kroger posted the information supplied to him by Lonsdale to Russia, in the form of microdots (pages reduced to the size of a pinhead) concealed inside parcels of books. Under the couple's kitchen floorboards a radio transmitter was hidden, capable of broadcasting as far as Moscow. It was a near-perfect set-up; their neighbours were completely unaware of what was going on.

Though Houghton never met the Krogers, he had dealt with other agents before he began working with Lonsdale in 1958. By this time Ethel and Harry were in the thick of their relationship, and Lonsdale soon suggested that she might be persuaded to become involved. 'She had access to material about NATO plans, British naval manoeuvres in conjunction with her allies, and other activities', Lonsdale wrote. This material would be of 'considerable value'.

Lonsdale was introduced to Ethel in 1960 as Commander Alec Johnson of the US Navy. His habit of chewing gum must have helped to convince her of his nationality. He said he was acting as go-between in an exchange of information between the US and the Royal Navy, but had difficulty in persuading some of the latter to supply any. Ethel apparently swallowed this tale and agreed to assist. It's likely that any money paid for her information went straight to Harry, who confessed in his autobiography, 'I conned Ethel'. She was charmed too by Lonsdale, who thought her 'a nice woman', and she obligingly borrowed secret Admiralty green-covered test papers for copying. This was not difficult for her to do, as security at the UDE was very lax, and registering the papers was a part of her job.

Though Ethel seems to have been discreet; Harry's lavish spending led to his downfall and that of his girlfriend, together with Lonsdale and the Krogers. Suspicions had been alerted in the UDE about Harry's activities, and he and Gee were being carefully watched. A near-neighbour of Harry's, Cyril Boggust, who worked at Redlands garage, was also a special constable. He kept a careful weekly log of Houghton's movements to or from the house. Papers released under the Fifty Year Rule in 2017 show the lengths to which the authorities went to entrap Houghton (code-named REVERBERATE) and, to a lesser extent, since she was thought to be an ill-educated woman, Gee, whose code-name was TRELLIS.

The end came on January 7th 1961. Houghton and Gee met Lonsdale (code-named LAST ACT) in London on Waterloo Road. They strolled along together, and Gee handed a shopping basket over to Lonsdale as they walked. As soon as the exchange had taken place, the police moved in to arrest them all. The Krogers (MR & MRS KILLJOY) were arrested later that same day. They were charged with 'conspiring together and with other persons unknown for purposes prejudicial to the safety or interest of the state to communicate to other persons information which might be directly or indirectly useful to an enemy'.

Inside Ethel's raffia bag a pile of the test papers was found, along with a tin of film containing 350 confidential pictures of warships. Lonsdale had a large sum of money in his pockets, in both sterling and dollars. When he was arrested, Houghton for once told the truth: 'I have been a bloody fool,' he said. Ethel however insisted that she had 'done nothing wrong'. All five pleaded not guilty. Lonsdale flatly refused to give evidence, a stance he maintained throughout the trial. Houghton made a statement exonerating Ethel, and claiming that both of them had been taken in by 'Alec Johnson'. Three days after his arrest he offered to turn Queen's Evidence, which – had his offer been accepted – would have freed him, but not his girlfriend.

The British Government decided to use the proceedings as anti-Russian propaganda, and ensured that the trial was given maximum publicity. On March 13th it opened in the No 1 court of the Old Bailey. This was the first case involving 'illegal residents' – that is, spies who operated in a foreign country without the cover of an embassy.

Oddly, the case was described in court documents as that of 'Miss Gee and others'. The press were certainly interested in her: a well-groomed spinster who had gone astray. She was remarkably calm (Lonsdale thought that she 'lacked imagination'). According to journalists Bulloch and Miller, compared with Houghton, Bunty Gee 'emerged as the stronger character. It became plain as she went on that she was not as dim-witted as she was apparently trying to appear, and that she had not played a completely subsidiary role in the spy-ring'. Another observer of the trial, Rebecca West, sensed a suppressed anger in her, a 'rage felt by people who think that society has given them no opportunities to use their ability or be honoured for it'. At one point in the proceedings she tapped a pencil on the ledge of the dock to attract the judge's attention. She had been prudent about money, and large sums in cash, savings certificates and shares were found in her bedroom. Money had been left to her by her father, and most of the investments dated from that earlier time. The police, however, suspected that at least some of the stash came from Lonsdale. Whatever the truth of this, she seems to have agreed to become a spy for love of Harry.

In a newspaper interview shortly after the trial, under the headline 'Love Made Me a Spy', Gee explained how she felt about Harry. During their evenings at the Elm Tree she would sit and admire her lover. 'There at the bar with his friends, local businessmen, wealthy farmers and professional men, Harry was a dominant figure.'

Harry himself, in the tangle of lies which formed his defence, declared that he had been blackmailed into giving away secrets. He had been beaten up in his caravan at Church Ope – but had appeared at work the next day without any signs of bruising. No one in court, Gordon Lonsdale wrote, showed any inclination to believe his tales.

Neither the Krogers nor Lonsdale went into the witness box, though Lonsdale made a statement in an attempt to exonerate the Krogers. This failed. All five were found guilty; Lonsdale was sentenced to twenty-five years, the Krogers to twenty years, and Houghton and Gee to fifteen years each.

None of the group served a full sentence. In 1965 Lonsdale was exchanged for the British businessman Greville Wynne, and the Krogers were released in 1969 in exchange for lecturer Gerald Brooke. Shortly afterwards Houghton and Gee were let out on parole, with an eager band of journalists in pursuit.

Ethel Gee was released from Styal Open Prison on May 12th 1970. On her release, she refused to speak, but obligingly posed for photographers. A picture in the *Daily Telegraph* on the following day shows her tucking into gammon, eggs and salad – while refusing potatoes – on her way home to Portland. On May 14th she was reported as saying that she did not want to see Harry Houghton again.

This resolution, if such it was, did not last for long. Shortly afterwards the pair met again, and were seen sharing afternoon tea at the Burley Manor Hotel in the New Forest. 'Miss Gee', the *Daily Telegraph* reported, 'drank three glasses of sherry and Mr Houghton [an unspecified number of] ginger beer shandies'.

Gee showed no signs of remorse for her actions. Her lack of shame was astonishing. On her return home to Portland, she was accosted by a man who called her a traitor. 'Scum', she retorted. Houghton, too, on his release from Maidstone Prison told a reporter 'If I weren't on probation I'd knock your bloody head off' – though he did express regret for having involved Ethel in the espionage. 'As long as I live', he said, 'my objective is to love and cherish Miss Gee'. She evidently forgave him – what else could she do? – and the couple were married in April 1971.

*

Years later, accounts of the doings of the Portland Spy Ring have a period feel about them. The Krogers' bungalow was in leafy Ruislip, a part of John Betjeman's Metroland. His poem 'Middlesex', published in 1954, saw the town as an old-fashioned place of rather affected gentility.

Gaily into Ruislip Gardens
Runs the red electric train,
With a thousand Ta's and Pardon's
Daintily alights Elaine;
Hurries down the concrete station
With a frown of concentration,
Out into the outskirt's edges
Where a few surviving hedges
Keep alive our lost Elysium – rural Middlesex again.

The Krogers seem to have fitted snugly into this background, and the tools of espionage discovered in their home perfectly matched their genteel domestic surroundings. There was a 'Three Roses' tin of talcum powder, found to have secret compartments; Russian signal plans in the cavity of a table lighter, and a false torch which housed papers. The paraphernalia of spying was poetic in its ingenuity.

And then there was Harry – a man who resembled a seedy stage drunk. After the trial, a Naval Intelligence officer was heard to remark, 'If we sacked every drunkard in Portland, we should have no staff', so Houghton must have fitted in easily. His movements outside work resembled one gigantic pub crawl. In Castletown, close to his workplace, he drank at the Breakwater Hotel, a pub in the harbour street lined with public houses (now mostly closed) which also served as brothels. He regularly drank Guinness in the early evening at his local, the New Inn, just round the corner from his house in Meadow View Road. He also drank at the Crown in Puncknowle (the coastal strip behind Chesil Bank is well-supplied with watering-holes). Gordon

Lonsdale twice visited him in Dorset, and on the second occasion they met at the Junction Hotel in Dorchester. On trips to London, to deliver information, Houghton often drank at the Bunch of Grapes in Knightsbridge.

On Tuesday and Wednesday evenings, his choice was the Elm Tree in Langton Herring, a public house which was very popular with Naval officers. He brought generous rounds of Scotch for chance acquaintances – and even though he did not realise it – for Special Branch officers who were following him. Ethel was usually at his side, though he sometimes took other women instead. He was not faithful to her: somewhat hypocritically, Lonsdale wrote that

Harry Houghton, Ethel Gee and the Renault Dauphine.

he had tried to stop Houghton chasing 'every bit of crumpet' he encountered.

Although his love of drink was one of the reasons he was selected as spy material, it also proved to be a drawback. (Lonsdale concluded that his recruitment had been a mistake and suspected that he would 'change sides at the drop of a hat'.) Houghton had several times been fined for dangerous driving. His car, an off-white Renault Dauphine (subsidised by his spying activities) was well-known to the police, who must have often witnessed him weaving along the pitch-dark lanes. He escaped arrest for drunken driving only because the police were biding their time, waiting until evidence of his espionage activities had been fully gathered.

Reports on the later life of Mr and Mrs Houghton generally conclude that the couple 'died in obscurity' in Poole. (Ethel died in 1984 and Harry in 1985.) If their spying activities had not been brought to a halt, they could have caused serious harm, and the names of Houghton and Gee still retain a tinge of infamy. (The film *Ring of Spies*, first released in 1964, is a fast-paced, grainy and atmospheric account of events, which investigates their relationship and motives. It has recently been re-mastered.) But there is one place where they are perhaps best remembered – and that is the Elm Tree pub in Langton Herring. Visitors come from far and wide for the chance to sit in the shady settle by the inglenook fireplace, where the shoddy couple enjoyed their regular evening drinks.

Song

Unusually for an English village, Langton Herring does not have a war memorial. This is because it is one of the 'Thankful Villages' (the only example in Dorset). The term was coined by the topographical writer, Arthur Mee, in his book *Enchanted Land* (1936) to describe the fifty-four villages in the country where all of the men who served in the First World War survived the fighting. Even more unusually, Langton Herring is among the far fewer number of villages which were 'Doubly Thankful', because they suffered no casualties in the Second World War either.

As part of a musical project, singer and songwriter Darren Hayman visited all of the Thankful Villages in 2015, and composed a song or individual tune for each one of them. Langton Herring's song was a lament for the boys killed in a terrible accident in the village in 1832.

Close by Langton Cross are the remains of a lime kiln, which was built in about 1830. Here the village boys used to play, daring one another to run across the top layer of limestone in the kiln, which was four and a half feet high. At five o'clock one afternoon, when only the bottom layer of stones was in place, four young boys – the two eldest were eight years old – climbed down on to the heated stones and were immediately overcome by the pungent fumes. Their names were Charles Vivian, Henry Mowlam, Richard Mowlam and John Hardy.

The first person who tried to rescue them was himself almost suffocated by the fumes. A surgeon was sent out from Abbotsbury, and the Rector of Langton Herring came to their aid – but all was in vain.

The boys' funeral was a momentous occasion. Eighteen children, dressed in white, carried their coffins to a single grave, marked by a plain wooden cross. In 1992 the cross was replaced by a stone to commemorate 'The Lime Kiln Disaster'. During the preparatory digging for the new monument a white stone angel with a broken wing was unearthed, and is now on display in the church. The gravestone bears the words:

REMEMBER / John Hardy / aged 7 /
Henry Mowlam / aged 8 / Richard Mowlam /
aged 6 / Charles Vivian / aged 8 / who died together /
in 1832 at play / in the village lime kiln.

The inscription ends with the words MEMOR ESTO BREVIS AEVI, which means 'Remember how short life is'. (This saying is often used on sundials as a *memento mori.*) In his song in memory of the four boys, whose lives were cut so tragically short, Darren Hayman changes the scene of the accident to the Chesil shore. The story is told in a haunting, breathless chant.

Run to the beach
Hide from the winds

Four boys dead in the kiln.
March in the sunlight
Kneel in the church
Eighteen children in white.

The accident has Biblical echoes too. In the Apocryphal 'Song of the Three Holy Children' three boys are cast into a 'burning fiery furnace' where their figures are then seen walking. Mercifully, they are saved from destruction when a fourth figure, an Angel, descends to smite 'the flame of the fire out of the oven'. These resonances, and Hayman's refining of the accident to the barest of bare bones, have together transformed the Langton Herring Lime Kiln Disaster from village history into folklore.

*Langton Cross (*Mick Orr*).*

Water Power

High up on Burton Bradstock's North Hill stands the broken carapace of another lime kiln, one of the chain along the coast from Burton to Swyre, to Puncknowle and to Langton Herring. The redundant kiln on North Hill met an ignominious end when it was appropriated by the Rural District Council for use as the local rubbish dump. North Hill also has an open reservoir, concealed in dense scrub, which was abandoned after the body of a woman was discovered, lying face downwards in its waters. She too had come to an unhappy end.

Another landmark on North Hill was a large cider press among the apple orchards – the *buddery dore* trees. This press was housed in a stone building to which the farmer, James Browne, gave the unlikely name of 'Cowper's Lodge' because he was a great admirer of the poems and hymns of the melancholy eighteenth century poet William Cowper.

In 1948, Browne set a stone in the south wall of the building, carved with the following sombre verses, which bear no reference to the building's contents. They were only just decipherable when they were transcribed by historian Maurice Ouseley for his unpublished (and undated) work on Burton Bradstock. The stone was last seen in a nearby garden.

COWPER'S LODGE

Oh for a lodge in some vast wilderness,
Some boundless contiguity of shade,
Where rumour of oppression and deceit,
Of unsuccessful or successful war,
Might never reach me more! My ear is pained,
My soul is sick with every day's report
Of wrong and outrage with which earth is filled.

William Cowper, 'A Time-Piece'

Over the years, gallons of cider have been made in Burton Bradstock. Cider was produced all around the village, in the old Dove and other inns and on the farmsteads. Drinking was a popular pastime. At the end of the nineteenth century there were thirteen public houses in village, though many of them must have been tiny cottage rooms, where cider was drunk and cares forgotten.

A poem by local writer Douglas Northover tells how on one occasion the drink was put to a more unexpected use. 'The Cyder Flood' is the story of a summer drought in Burton Bradstock, a drought so severe that cherished garden plants were wilting with thirst. Desperate, one of the gardeners watered her flowers with a cask of her husband's cider – to astonishing effect.

Among the plants it soaked and oozed,
The herbs were first to get quite boozed.
The marjoram jumped from the ground,
With the thyme danced round and round...

...people came from all around
To see this quite amazing ground
Where drunken plants could dance and play
And alcohol just ruled the day.

On hearing the news, the parish council, the National Trust and the local tourist board all tried to join in, but the villagers were determined to keep the secret of their success to themselves. However, when it began to rain, the boozy flower show was washed utterly away.

It was cider which fuelled the farming and fishing that provided most of the employment along the Chesil. Choices of work were historically few, but the people of Burton Bradstock were perhaps fortunate in having an extra source of income. They could grow and process flax.

Flax and hemp will only grow under certain conditions, in areas with rich soils and a warm climate. Both plants flourished around Burton Bradstock and nearby Bridport, and also in South Somerset at places like West Coker and Crewkerne. Of the two plants, hemp is the taller and coarser, and was used for rope-making. For eight hundred years its cultivation made Bridport the main centre for this trade, giving the town long-lasting links with the Navy. In 1211, King John ordered that Bridport should make 'many ropes for ships both large and small'. Ropewalks were set up in and around Burton Bradstock in the sixteenth century until an Act of Parliament in 1530 forbade rope-making and selling of hemp within five miles of Bridport to protect the town's trade.

Flax, which is a smaller plant with finer fibres, was used for making sailcloth and linen: the turning of flax into twine was a cottage industry until the nineteenth century. The plants were grown in the village at Badden's Close, Lower Traces, Brighton Moor and up on Bennet's Hill, or were delivered to the villagers from elsewhere in the district. Preparing the flax was a long and arduous process. The plants were pulled from the ground just before the purplish-blue flowers began to fade. They were then beaten, and the fallen seeds were collected for the next sowing, or made into linseed oil.

Then came the 'retting', when the cut flax, now a dirty grey, was laid out and soaked in water – either in the dew of the fields, which took about twenty days, or in retting ponds, which took around fifteen. The flax was soaked until the pithy core had rotted away. (There was a retting pond in a Burton Bradstock field, quite close to one of the mills.)

The retted flax was beaten yet again, to separate the unwanted woody parts from the stalks. Even before industrialisation this was done by machine, using the power of a water wheel to trip a line of metal stamps which crushed the stems. Young boys had the task of placing the fibres under the stamps (risking the loss of their fingers in the process).

In the next stage, 'scutching' (or scraping), the woody parts were removed. The flax was then ready for 'hackling', when the flax was repeatedly combed, a process which removed shorter or coarser fibres, and left the flax in long hair-like hanks – like horses' tails – which the spinners looped around their waists. At every stage in the refining, the fibres became softer.

For spinning, each family had its own 'walk': a narrow passage, which could be up to one hundred metres long, and was often open to the sky. At one end of the walk was a large wheel with a pole handle, turned by the children of the family. On the outer side of the wheel was a ring of hooks which revolved as the wheel was turned, and to which the spinner attached a portion of the fibre. The spinner then walked backwards, paying out the fibre, which was caught on the hooks and twisted into yarn. The girls and women who acted as the spinners moved up and down, down and up the walks, covering many miles a day, twisting the twine into yarn.

Yarn-making, then, was a long and convoluted set of procedures, from beating to combing to – above all – the twisting of the twine. It even had its own tongue-twister, according to the writer Eden Phillpotts.

When a twister, a twisting, will twist him a twist,
With the twisting his twist, he the twine doth untwist,
But if one of the twines of the twist doth untwist,
The twine that untwisteth, untwisted the twist.
Untwisting the twine that entwineth between,
He twists with his twister the two in a twine.
Then, twice having twisted the twines of his twine,
He twisteth the twine he had twined in twine.
The twain, that in twining before in the twine,
As twines were entwisted, he now doth untwine,
'Twixt the twain intertwisting a twine more between.

Eden Phillpotts, from *The Spinners*

Phillpotts was a prolific author, famous in the day for his novels set on Dartmoor, the most notable of which was *Widecombe Fair*. He was also the writer of a group of novels about various rural industries, such as pottery and paper-making. In 1911 he stayed in Burton Bradstock, where he visited the flax-spinning mill. His novel *The Spinners*, published in 1918, is set in Bridetown, an old name for the village.

Phillpotts evidently studied the twine-making processes very closely by becoming, like his main character, Raymond Ironsyde, a trainee worker in the spinning mill, which he described as 'a heterogeneous pile of dim, dun colours and irregular roofs huddled together with silver-bright excrescences of corrugated iron'. He also absorbed the sounds of the building and its smells. The storehouse 'reeked with that fat heavy odour peculiar to hemp and flax', while in the mill 'two sounds deafened an unfamiliar ear: a steady roar, deep and persistent, and through it, like a staccato pulse, a louder, more painful, more penetrating din. The bass to this harsh treble arose from humming belts and running wheels; the crash that punctuated their deep-mouthed riot broke from the drawing heads of the machines'.

He observed the yarn-making process in great and choreographed detail: in particular the 'high task' of the spinners. These young women 'seemed to twinkle here, there and everywhere in a corybantic measure as they served the shouting and insatiable monsters that turned hemp and flax to yarn'. Phillpotts' heroine Sabina is the most skilful of the spinners, the queen of the mill.

Phillpotts was concerned about the treatment of the workers, most especially the children at the mill. While he was in Burton Bradstock, he wrote to his daughter Adelaide about the eleven girls who were employed in the spinning factory. 'They work ten hours a day and only skilled spinners get much more than a penny or two pence an hour. Yet some of their work involves much cleverness and skill and a great deal of physical energy, for those who watch the spindle have to be on their feet dancing about all the time.' Conditions were slowly improving, but still had a long way to go.

Phillpotts' novel is set in a period long after the mill had become mechanised. The great change had come in 1803, when Richard Roberts took over an old flour mill on the banks of the River Bride, between his home at Grove House and Bredy Farm. Roberts's grandparents had moved from Wales to nearby Chilcombe, high above the sea, while his father Francis settled at Bredy Farm on the River Bride. Richard, his second son, prudently married a rich widow, Martha Hoskins, who held Burton Farm and had built Grove House, a charming village residence with a mulberry tree in the garden. The marriage produced five children, but it was not a love match. In later years the couple split up when Roberts moved to Girt House in the village. Afterwards they met only briefly, at church services on Sundays.

Roberts' first venture in Burton Bradstock had come in 1794, when he built a small water-powered flax spinning mill below the church. Another mill, with its own water wheel, had been added by 1822. In 1803 – as a plaque on the building confirms – he built the Grove Mill, which was a swingling mill, where the flax or hemp fibres were separated. This mill was probably used until it became common practice to buy imported flax, which had already been prepared for spinning.

Roberts' Grove Mill was powered by steam, and its introduction made cottage industry in Burton and the surrounding villages unprofitable. The villagers were obliged to work in the mill, losing their independence, and being ruled by time, in the shape of the 'curfew bell'.

Much of the Industrial Revolution had passed Dorset by. It was a county of vast agricultural estates, with no coal (although it is now known to be rich in oil) and only small quantities of iron ore. There were no canals. Apart from the stone quarries of Portland and Purbeck, the industries were small-scale and rural, using local raw materials like lime, ball clay, wheat for milling and barley for beer-making. The industries were powered by wind, water and animals – until the introduction of steam.

In 1811, Roberts began to build another spinning mill at the Grove. He was prospering, but – when for instance his workers were bringing in the harvest, or there was a sighting of fish out at sea – he was sometimes short of labour. He applied to various West Country workhouses for children. He wrote that he preferred to employ girls between the ages of eight and ten, when they were at their most obedient and industrious. He promised to take care of them, attending to their 'food and raiment and morals'. Roberts was no worse than many another employer, but like them, he would turn a girl out when her period of employment was over, and she would be left to fend for herself. In *The Spinners* a character remarks on child employment in those earlier times. 'Think of the little children, too, and how they were made to work. Think of them and feel your heart ache.'

Roberts was said to produce thirty varieties of linen and claimed to have the use of two hundred looms for weaving.

The surviving two volumes of his letter books show his attention to detail in his business dealings. He seems, though, to have been his own worst enemy, as his daughter Edith breathlessly remarked.

> He was very clever, very fond of new things, deeply interested in every new discovery in science and fond of art, very musical played violin and flute and had a chamber organ, trained the Church choir, very fond of Scotchmen had two as overseers…a great speculator, at one time having made £2,000 a year but lost it by speculation always having new machinery, a great lawyer, always in lawsuits for the pleasure of it and settling the disputes of all his neighbours.

Unfortunately none of his children inherited his drive or his flair, though two of his sons, like many other young men along the Chesil, joined the Navy. His second son Richard was a midshipman who served under local hero Captain Hardy on board the *Victory* at the Battle of Trafalgar in 1805, and later drew a detailed plan of the battle. The tradition of Naval service was strong in the village, and after Richard's death a copy of the anthem of the 'Loyal Volunteers of Burton Bradstock' was found among his papers.

Burton's sons were always brave
On the land or ocean,
Ready for to kill or save,
When honour's the promotion.

*

After Roberts' death, his mills went through various incarnations. The Mill Street spinning factory was burnt down in 1874, after the tow in a cording machine burst into flames. The factory chimney, which dominated the village, survived the fire, and the mill was rebuilt by Lord Rivers. It ended up as a vehicle repair shop and caravan store. By 1881, Grove Mill had been taken over by the Rendall family, becoming a grinding mill and bakery. It was sold in 1958 and the bakery was closed.

Flax mills underwent a brief revival during the Second World War. In 1939, Rolf Gardiner began flax-growing and processing at Slape Mill, below Netherbury. A once-prosperous twine mill, Slape was by then 'in a state of melancholy decay', though still lushly-supplied with water power. Gardiner restored the derelict mill, adding 'two magnificent Dutch barns' and providing a hostel for the workers. These included a reliable group from Fontmell Magma (where Gardiner planned to form a rural industries co-operative), with other experienced flax workers, and a collection of agricultural labourers and girls in flight from 'the old-fashioned Christian home', all of whom were more interested in 'their pay-packets and their cider' than in their work.

There was a sharp divide between the methods recommended by the Ministry of Supply and Gardiner's own practices. In Fontmell he had 'experimented with a horse-pulled flax harvesting machine'. Regardless of the small hilly fields and the damp climate, the Ministry was intent on mass-production, and the use of 'green flax': de-seeding by machine and by-passing the retting process. This method was deplored by Gardiner and did not work well at Slape. He wrote that 'The lovely flax was tossed about from process to process like so much hay'.

This clash of cultures was not a success. Gardiner went on to a further experiment at Lopen in South Somerset, and Slape Mill became for a while a maggot farm, malodorous and mucky, and later a wrecker's yard. Not much of it is left now. An immaculate group of houses surrounds a village green in the kind of silence which has become common in the Dorset countryside.

*

In Bridport Town Hall a series of highly-coloured paintings and murals are on permanent display. They were created by Francis ('Fra') Newbery, who studied at Bridport School of Art and in 1885 became director of Glasgow School of Art. One of the paintings shows the women of a local family net-braiding together in a cottage room, a skill which was a useful source of extra income. A little girl is loading the braiding needle with twine for her grandmother to knot into a mesh. (The net maker was Mrs Bagg of Myrtle Cottage in nearby Loders, who explained the process to Newbery.) The knot she is using is a sheet bend, which is tied around the fingers of the left hand: the braider then passes the needle through the knot to secure it. The technique resembles knitting with only one needle: the chosen number of meshes are cast on, and can be increased or decreased as required. Each village had its own speciality: in Burton Bradstock some of the finer meshes were produced.

Net-braiding is a craft which requires few tools, and allows for some freedom of movement, as Gordon Beckles described in 1953.

> She might be in her kitchen, or tending the cattle, or helping in the fields or just sitting before her cottage door, but wherever she might be she would likely have near at hand a 'ran' or measure of twine, a block of wood called a 'lace' and a wooden needle shaped like a dagger with a tongue running down its centre. She chats away to a neighbour in the next cottage similarly employed, and if there are any children in the picture...one can be sure that they too are braiding, so that it becomes second nature...

There are photographs of women at their cottage doors, some of them wearing their 'Burton bonnets'. Other braiders ventured further afield. Maurice Ouseley photographed women nonchalantly braiding on Chesil Bank. One of them is using her foot for the purpose. This does suggest though

*Net-braiding on Chesil Beach (*Maurice Ouseley*).*

that braiding was a never-ending task, but it did earn the cottage workers a welcome extra income, and gave them a certain degree of independence. Net-braiding has survived as a skill, but almost all the mills in the area have gone, converted like Slape into private housing.

Burton Bradstock is a handsome village, built in local stone, and is now a modish one. In its quiet centre there is neither sound nor sight of the sea, but water continues to make its power felt. Burton Bradstock has always been prone to flooding, which has been intensified by the sluices and leats constructed to help drive the mills: these have altered the river's course. Where the mouth of the Bride meets the Chesil at Freshwater the river becomes dammed with shingle which has to be cleared to let the water escape. Serious flooding occurs when the Bride meets a high tide which sweeps the shingle up into the river mouth, causing the Bride to back up. The sea rises above it, flooding the low-lying water meadows and pouring into the village. Despite flood warnings and renewed defences there is no sure way of preventing this happening. Floods and tempests, wind and weather, all define the Chesil coast.

Although it may once have stretched further, Chesil Bank now begins at Burton Bradstock. Here, the pebbles are miniature ones, like brown sugar crystals, and the Bank itself is scarcely discernible. The dramatic shrinking in size and height of the shingle from its triumphant peak at Portland makes Burton Bradstock seem more like the end of the Bank than its curious beginning.

Pebbles

Fleet means 'a run of water' and *chesil* means 'pebble': They are plain, no-nonsense words for a highly unusual pairing. Like flakes of snow, no two pebbles on Chesil Bank are identical – even though most of them are made from just one kind of stone, which is flint, or its close relation, chert. This stone has travelled westward from the flint-bearing chalk cliffs between Seaton and Sidmouth on the Devon coast.

Flint is pure silica, its pebbles are brown and grey. Flint is also as hard as steel, and so is resistant to being knocked into shape. But all pebbles are transient, even flint, and are remorselessly pounded by the waves into smaller and smaller particles. When flint breaks down into sand it is still 'sharp' as the granules persist in their angularity. But break it must. In 1962, a flint-knapping site was found on the Abbbotsbury shore, between the beach road and the pebbles. The flints had somehow been worked 'by a metal implement', into various tools, which were then used to make armlets out of the Kimmeridge shale found in nearby Portesham. The site is described as 'enigmatic', because it is difficult to date (though it is not as old as the prehistoric stone workings along the lagoon from Small Mouth to West Fleet).

The Cornish granite which is found in the shingle differs from most of the other pebbles in being of plutonic origin, meaning that it was formed under the earth.(Pluto was the Greek god of the Underworld.) Pumice comes from volcanoes in the Caribbean. Rarer pebbles found along the shingle may have been shed by some of the wrecks which line the bay. The pebbles were used as ballast, which would sink with the capsizing ships and their cargoes, eventually washing up along the shore. In this way pebbles from foreign lands were added to the more local mix. The magnetite (an iron ore also known as lodestone) found near Abbotsbury is believed to have come from the wreck of the SS *Dorothea*, which came to grief due to engine failure in 1914. There too, picnicking local families such as the Toms would look for 'that elusive stone called the "Abbotsbury Pebble". It had to be brown in colour, with green spots, no other colour would be allowed'.

Other much prized pebbles were those with a hole burrowed through them by the waves. Such stones were considered lucky. String was threaded through the holes, and pendant-like, they would be hung by a door, or on a fishing-boat.

All pebbles become more buoyant in the water, especially in salt water, just as swimmers do, making their bodies easier for the waves to shift. The long-shore drift of the waves is from west to east: the prevailing winds which drive the waves are from the south-west, so they often reach the shore obliquely. Only the fetch – the crest of the waves – is in motion, the deep waters below remain calm. Clarence Ellis in *Pebbles on the Beach* defines the fetch as 'the length of the stretch of wind-swept water over which waves travel. The longer the fetch, the larger the waves.'

After the waves have broken on the shore, their wash continues to surge up the beach, drawing the pebbles with it. The ensuing backwash drags them back down towards the sea. And so it goes on, without end.

Shaping and grading is a continuous process. The sea's action in grading the pebbles from the largest in the east to the smallest in the west can be difficult to spot, especially in the central section of Chesil Bank (even with the well-seasoned eye of a ship-wrecked sailor). But tests have shown that the old saying is true, as Clarence Ellis makes plain.

> Experiments with broken bricks have proved how inevitably and accurately the process of sorting goes on. Pieces of brick were chosen because they are easily distinguishable from the shingle. They were placed on the beach at various points between high and low-water mark. Every one of them in due course made its way to its appropriate place on the ridge, and lay side by side with pebbles of the same magnitude.

(Stranger still is the behaviour of the shingle in Lulworth Cove on the other side of Weymouth, where the larger pebbles gather in the centre, with the smaller pebbles at their sides.)

Abandoned by the waves, the beached pebbles glow like jewels, though even the rarest of them are of little monetary worth. However, until recently – and as they had been for centuries – the sand and shingle were valued as construction materials. Sand from Burton Bradstock was used in the building of Abbotsbury Abbey, in about 1040. In the twentieth century there were extractions of around 10,000 tonnes at the Chiswell end of the Bank. Most of the removals took place between Abbotsbury and West Bay, from where it's estimated over one million tonnes of sand and shingle were lifted. In the 1950s a sand merchant called Geoffrey Good was using shire horses to collect the shingle in Burton Bradstock. Two-wheeled carts were used to carry the loads up the cliff track. The material was chosen according to the wind's direction: sand, when it was blowing from the west, and small pebbles in the east wind which washes them up. The shingle – pea-gravel – was used for water-purification, for pebble-dashing and for paving. Much of it was sent to Scotland by sea. At the Portland end of the Bank, it was used in the perfume-making process. Sand is used for building work, though the salt must first be washed out, or the sand will be unusable. Concrete made with unwashed sand will not set.

The process was not discontinued until the mid-1980s, when it became – somewhat belatedly – regarded as unsustainable. Removal of shingle caused damage to the cliffs, affecting their strength as sea-defences and causing erosion. It was also feared that extraction might be affecting Chesil Bank's ability to renew itself. The decision meant that this, the most harmful exploitation among so many over the centuries, was over. Chesil Bank is a landscape for which a balance now has to be maintained between conservation and the ever-growing needs of tourism: an industry which tends to kill the thing it loves.

The lives of the people along the Chesil have always been shaped by the sea, which is both a hostile and a fruitful presence. Behind the ever-shifting bank, the times are

*Sand extraction at West Bay (*Maurice Ouseley*).*

changing, but day and night the sounds the people hear remain the same. They hear the sound of the pebbles' grating roar, a dying rattle, they hear the ghostly sighing of the sea and the soft hiss of the water flowing like quicksilver through the shingle of the Bank. So much has happened here, and so much more has been forgotten.

What would the world be, once bereft
Of wet and of wildness? Let them be left,
O let them be left, wildness and wet;
Long live the weeds and the wilderness yet.

Gerard Manley Hopkins, 'Inversnaid'

East Cliff, West Bay (David Brown).

Afterword 1

An anonymous account, written on the blue lined paper much favoured by the Victorians, preserved in Dorset History Centre.

Short Notice of the Waters called the Fleet
In the County of Dorset

The Fleet is a long lagoon or inlet running eight miles up from Portland Mouth to Reed's End boathouse on the beach near Abbotsbury. It coasts the five manors of Wyke Regis, Chickerel, Fleet or Fleethouse, Langton Herring, and Abbotsbury. It is noted for a Decoy and Oysterbeds, but still more for a Swannery: all belonging to the Earl of Ilchester, as having been parcel of the rights and possessions of the late monastery of Abbotsbury. There is little fish in it except eels and flounders, and grey mullet. The water is salt or brackish throughout all its extent, and it is affected by tides from the East bay, while the waters of the West bay occasionally find their way over or through the pebbles of the Chesil Bank.

The Abbey of Abbotsbury was founded A D 1024 by Orc, steward to King Canute, and Tola his wife, under the special sanction of that Monarch, whose cross or mark is still on the original foundation Charter still extant. It was endowed with various gifts and immunities confirmed by Edward the Confessor, William the Conqueror, Henry 2nd, 3rd, and 6th, Edward 4th, and Richard 3rd, which privileges, together with the Abbey lands, were granted to Sir Giles Strangways by Henry the 8th, in 1544...

These grants comprehend all the royalties on land and on shore, the flight of swans, fishery, waters, and soil of the Fleet, expressly so given, as to include the power of drainage or embankment, flotsam, jetsam, *wreccum maris*, &c. &c.

Lord Ilchester is Lord of the Manors of the two extreme parishes on the Fleet waters, Abbotsbury and Wyke, and by all the Charters and confirmations both before and since the dissolution of the Monasteries, owner of the waters of the Fleet, along the shore of the intermediate parishes, and of the soil thereof, from end to end. This expression is explained in some of the later confirmations under Elizabeth or the Stuart Kings, by the term "these drowned lands known as East Flete and West Flete", a term well known as applied to the similarly situated fens in the Eastern counties which were beginning to be drained. That this was the view of the Crown in granting these confirmations is clear from the conditional imposition of a fine stipulated to be paid, in case such drainage took place but not otherwise. It was however attempted, under Sir John Strangways, who leased to one Fry, a bight or bay called Earbury, on the Langton shore, but the experiment failed. There are embankments still visible in Earbury bay, called to this day, Fry's works.

The depth of water, and other conditions topographical of the Fleet, may have been very different in former times to what they are at present. In early days, Portland is given as an island, a channel cutting it off from the spit of pebbles called the Chesil bank, which has now long united it to the main land. What effect such an opening, co-existing with the present Portland mouth of the Fleet, which is never likely to have been closed, might have had on the level of the Fleet waters, it is difficult to estimate.

The Fleet seems to have been considered as a marsh land rather than an estuary, and as such had its own sea-shore (the Chesil – Kiesel, German, a flint) which carried with it all the maritime, or admiralty rights before mentioned, as granted to the Abbey by King Canute, confirmed by his successors, transferred to Sir Giles Strangways by Henry the Eighth, and by his successors again confirmed to the family, and now residing in the Earl of Ilchester.

Afterword 2

The Compost Heap
Notes of a Lecture on Food Production

By A M Curtis, Warden C C C

Choose a waste bit of the garden, about 25ft. x 15ft.to give space for three heaps, 7ft. x 4ft. with intervals for turning.

Collect all vegetable refuse, weeds, clippings, grass mowing, prunings, etc. Thick stalks and roots should be chopped.

Spread 6 inches of this 7ft. x 4ft., but do not beat or tread it down. Damp it thoroughly. Then spread kitchen garbage and lavatory waste. Cover lightly with peat mould or fine dry earth, enough to make a decent appearance – say 2 inches.

Repeat till heap is 4ft. high and squarely shaped, not in a peak. Water gently with bath, kitchen, laundry waste or rain water once a day, taking care not to throw it into the centre, but thoroughly wetting the sides. After three or four days push an iron road into the middle, leave it 5 minutes, take it out, and, if hot to the hand, fermentation is active.

If not, add more water if dry, or loosen to aerate if too close.

After two weeks, turn into next vacant space, top to base, outside to inside, any hard fibre being placed at the bottom of the heap.

Two weeks later turn back to first position. Leave for 4 weeks and turn again for third and last time. Leave again for four weeks; when it is ready for use and should be taken and dug in at once where wanted, or its value will be lessened by every day's delay.

While 1st heap is fermenting a second and third can be started.

Make and leave for 2 weeks.
Turn and leave for 2 weeks.
Turn and leave for 4 weeks.
Turn and leave for 4 weeks
12 weeks in all.

Pea and bean haulm can be used, but should be cut off, *not* pulled out, because the nitrogenous roots must be left in the ground as fertiliser.

The following are points usually neglected by gardeners and farmers for want of care, common sense, and chemical knowledge – with bad results. Quite possible for an expert to inspect a compost heap and not detect the errors in its making.

Never to use lime in the process. It should be added to the soil 3-6 months *after* the compost has been dug in.

Never to empty kitchen refuse or lavatory pails in a lump, but scatter it on top of the heap evenly.

Never to leave waste uncovered to attract rats and lose nitrogen by evaporation. Put on a thin layer of fine earth or peat-mould or grass cuttings, any vegetable clippings, weeds, etc.

It is the duty of every householder to destroy the National Enemy RAT which costs the nation one hundred million pounds sterling every year. *Rodine* put down *once a month* keeps them away, and a gin is better than the wire trap. Many a housewife picks thyme, parsley, mint, etc., from her herb-patch that *looks* as clean as a new pin, but a microscope would show that the filthy body of a rat had run through it in the night.

To build heap not less than 7 ft. x 4ft.x 4ft. or temperature will be too low, and weed seeds will not be destroyed.

Never to beat down the heap, but to leave it loose for aeration. It must *not* be firm and tight. To crush it down with a spade is folly.

Water *sides*, not centre. Sprinkle top.

In turning, put top and sides to bottom and take out hard woody fibre for base of next heap. Fresh waste can be added for first month only.

When 12 weeks are up, compost must never be allowed to stand "till wanted". It *must* be wheeled to the land and dug in at once, *not* kept in heaps for sun, wind and rain to destroy its value.

Careful note of time must be kept, that each stack may receive its turning at the right intervals.

Lavatory pails must be of galvanised iron or enamel, but if enamel becomes chipped it is useless, as the pail will be fouled, and become impossible to clean. Each pail must have its well-fitting cover, but the cover should not be taken out of the lavatory. Each pail must be scoured with hard brush and water after daily emptying. Fluid and solid waste can be in the same pail and "peat mould" is the best deodorizer and fertilizer. Supplied in sacks or in bulk by Eclipse Peat Co., Ashcott, Somerset. Beneficial in itself for either stiff or light soils. For plans of lavatory for numbers, at least cost and quickest working, see Dr. Poore's illustrations in "Rural Hygiene", last edition. A most valuable book, out of print, but a few copies can be obtained second-hand. One man or woman can manage ten lavatory pails easily in an hour a day, if they are arranged with hatches at the back for taking out the pails and putting in the peat. Everyone should do the whole process for 12 weeks for thorough training. Chemical "antiseptics" must *never* be used, nor burnt earth.

N.B. Thin toilet paper is best, and should be burnt before adding the shovelful of peat mould or fine earth, otherwise the pail fills too quickly and the paper *may* blow off the compost heap. Hair combings, shaving paper, and any other effects of personal hygiene should also be burnt in the lavatory pail before covering with earth. In this way everything returns to the land for beneficent use instead of being poured into rivers and sea to pollute the fish and foul the waters, tainting wells on its way and causing epidemics of disease, with vast expenditure of public money, and far less good fertilisers are brought in at great cost from abroad.

Wood ash should not be used in compost, as its potash content is spoiled by wet. It should be kept in a dry *covered* dust-bin until wanted; then put in a seed trench and covered with earth, or dug into fruit-trees, etc., but never allowed to be rained on before being dug in and well covered.

Excrement from diseased bodies, human or animal, should *never* be used for compost, nor dug into the soil. It should always be put into a pit removed from food-growing land and covered thoroughly with *quicklime*. Food is unfit to be eaten by man or beast when grown in ground contaminated by the excreta of cancerous, tubercular, syphilitic or other diseased bodies. The dung of animals suffering from anthrax is used as fertilizer on farms, the droppings of diseased poultry are used as plant-food, and even the blood of the slaughter house is recommended as excellent stimulant for tomatoes! Many a life has been lost from tetanus caused by disease-infected earth. The hygiene of Moses is ages in advance of our modern "science".

No man or animal should ever eat the crops grown on sewage farms. Tomato seeds will pass through a malignantly diseased body and grow and fruit as if they were clean and wholesome, but their tissues are not fit for food.

Moses would think the "Christian" men and women of to-day quite mad if he saw what they eat and drink. He would not believe that they had ever heard of the Laws of God.

Burnt or sterilized earth should not be used for lavatory pails. Nor must any disinfectants be used. Living earth (i.e. with bacteria) or humus such as peat mould is the right thing, for the chemical action of transmutation. Soapy water from bathroom and laundry, and fatty water from kitchen can be used with profit; also waste paper after rotting it in a tub. Coal ash is of little use and is better kept for making paths. The waste of every living creature is enough to provide fertilization for its food supply when the waste is intelligently used. But man interferes with the marvellous cycle of Nature in which nothing is useless; and by breaking her rhythm he makes the discord of disease for himself and all below him. The foolish godson of Queen Elizabeth who invented the "water closet" has been a malefactor to the race: and the County Councils and their Sanitary Surveyors and Medical Officers perpetuate his evil folly instead of learning from Moses the true hygiene. The value in pounds sterling of the "waste" cast into the sea during the last 400 years in England alone would stagger the imagination. So ignorant and bigoted is local government that only those fortunate enough to live in rural areas outside the radius of sewerage can have an intelligent and wholesome system: but they will have to pay as high a rate as if they had the stupid town system. Individuals can discreetly instal Mosaic sanitation in their own homes if they have big gardens and know how to manage all the details in the right way. But they must leave the W.C. system untouched for the Sanitary Inspector, and under cover of it go their own better way, by having some well-ventilated dressing-room or big cupboard or garden shed fitted with a movable pail and seat, with a box or pail of peat with a shovel, within easy reach of a corner of the garden for 2 or 3 compost heaps, to one of which the lavatory pails would be taken every day.

A rain tank and brush handy to the heap is a saving of labour and time for rinsing out the pail and adding the water to the heap. I have done every detail myself when 70 years of age, including the making and 3 turnings of the compost heap single handed, and there is nothing unpleasant or difficult about it. At no time is there any smell of rottenness, or of ordure, if the right method is followed, as here advised after years of practical working.

Afterword 3

George Davey

George Davey, who died in 2010, aged 101, was a banker mason, producing technical drawings for stone buildings. His great loves were Portland, poetry, and his family. His poems are rapid slide-shows of the island he knew so well.

Chesil Memories

I often think I'd like to meet,
Those folk who walked that busy street,
The Chesil folk, of days gone by,
Who linger in my memory.

Who is that by the Pump so tall.
His house is there, by yonder wall,
I know him by his bowed down head,
It must be dear old Father Fred.

I see a girl, who once I knew,
And Wabbler, called her Betty Blue
There's Sunny with his well-tanned face
He's proved to be of noble race.

Now Mary Jane and sister Sue
'Tis said their rates are overdue,
They're going out to Jacob's Well,
The water's turned off so they tell.

That little man called Frenchy Bill,
Do you recall his voice so shrill,
See General and his brother Dap,
Who always walks behind a lap.

A blind man, too, who mends a net,
His name this moment, I forget,
He knits so fast with no delay,
Ah, now I know, it's Mr. Way.

There's Mrs. Byatt on the Beach,
Who lives within the wild waves' reach,
Just over by the fishing-store,
She cooks her crabs there by the score.

For Carnival the men they meet,
To form a Jazz Band in the Street.
The man in front is Mr. May,
In Policeman's clothes, he leads the way.

That must be Lily over there,
In Gypsy dress, I do declare,
And Nellie, dressed in Gingham Gown,
Parades with them right through the Town.
In Chesil, here was aid and more,

Should babe be knocking at the door,
The kindly hand was always there,
To help the neighbour make repair.

And with the homes brought to the floor,
I wonder what there is in store,
Will others now, with friendly grace,
Respond, to fill this well loved place.

GEORGE DAVEY

Bibliography

Magpie-like, I have gathered information for this book from all manner of places, people, maps and papers. The more important sources are listed below.

Every attempt has been made to trace copyright holders, and any omission is unintentional.

Main sources

Falkner, John Meade, *Moonfleet,* Edward Arnold, 1898

Hutchins, John, *History and Antiquities of the County of Dorset*, 3rd edition, 4 vols, 1861–70

Proceeding of Dorset Natural History & Antiquarian Field Club (to 1928)

Proceedings of Dorset Natural History & Archaeological Society from1929

(both hereafter cited as *Proceedings*)

The Moons and the Fleet

Atkins, George, 'Discovering *Moonfleet*', Fleet church, undated

Barnes, William, *A Glossary of the Dorset Dialect*, Toucan Press, second edition 1970

Barnes, William Miles, 'Fleet Old Church and its Brasses', *Proceedings* 19, 1898

Clarke, Nigel J, *From Hope's Nose to St Alban's Head*, Nigel J Clarke, undated

Falkner, John Meade, *The Lost Stradivarius*, William Blackwood, 1895

Falkner, John Meade, *The Nebuly Coat*, Edward Arnold, 1903

Gardiner, Dorothy, *Companion into Dorset*, Methuen, 1937

Goodden, Wyndham, 'Report on Subterranean Passages in Fleet Churchyard', *Proceedings* 47, 1926

Guttridge, Roger, *Dorset Smugglers*, Dorset Publishing Company, 1984

Hardy, Florence, *Life of Thomas Hardy*, Macmillan, 1960

Kemp, John F, *The Book of Chesil Beach Dorset*, Nigel J Clarke, undated

Le Pard, Gordon, 'Gardens in the Sea?', Nautical Archaeological Society Newsletter, 2000

McEwan, Ian, *On Chesil Beach*, Cape, 2007

Miller, Alan J, 'The Mohuns of Hammoon and Fleet', *Dorset*, May 2001

Noble, Humphrey Brunel, *Life in Noble Houses*, undated

Pretor, Alfred, *Ronald and I*, Deighton Bell & Co, new edition 1901

Richardson, Nelson M, Report on the Fleet and Chickerell meeting, July 1897, *Proceedings* 19, 1898

Sack-Haunchwitz, Angela, 'Exploring Moonfleet', undated

Stevenson, Robert Louis, *Kidnapped*, Cassell 1886

Wilson, John Marius, *Imperial Gazeteer of England and Wales*, Fullarton & Co, 1880

Dorset History Centre:

Fleet House sale catalogue D599/A/28;

Papers of John Meade Falkner D/FAL/14

Fleet church guides, 1986; 1999
The History of Fleet House and Fleet Village Dorset, undated

Bexington-on-Sea

Collis, John Stewart, *Bound Upon a Course*, Sidgwick & Jackson, 1971
Cox, J Stevens, *Brief Notes on the History of West Bexington*, Toucan Press, 1969
Curtis, Adela, *The Compost Heap*, 1939
Curtis, Adela, *Divine Law of Marriage*, 1934
Curtis, Adela, *Dynamic Prayer*, 1940
Curtis, Adela, *Everyman's War*, 1941
Curtis, Adela, *In Praise of Littleness*, 1919/1946
Draper, Jo, 'Losing the Plot', *Dorset*, October 2001
Good, Ronald, *Lost Villages of Dorset*, Dovecote Press, 1979
Hardy, Thomas, *Collected Letters*, vol 6, Oxford University Press, 1987
Hardy, Thomas, *Complete Poems*, Macmillan, 1976
Huxley, Aldous, *Point Counter Point*, Chatto & Windus 1928
Ingrams, Richard, *John Stewart Collis*, Chatto & Windus 1986
Lawrence, D H, *Women in Love*, Secker, 1921
Lea, F A, *John Middleton Murry*, Methuen, 1959
Millgate, Michael, *Thomas Hardy*, Oxford University Press 1982
Moon, A A, 'Notes on the History and Architecture of West Bexington', 1979
Murry, John Middleton, *Between Two Worlds*, Cape 1935
Rudd, Chris, 'The Rustic Mystic of Burton Bradstock', *Dorset Year Book* 1985
Tomlinson, H M, 'Concerning Authors' Cottages No 7', *The Countryman Book*, Odhams Press 1948

Tomlinson, H M, *A Mingled Yarn*, Duckworth, 1953

Tomlinson, H M, 'Things Seen on the Autumnal Dorset Coast', *The Times*, November 3rd 1955

Tomlinson, H M, *Thomas Hardy*, Crosby Gaige, 1929

Tomlinson, H M, *The Wind is Rising*, Hodder and Stoughton, 1941

Worpole, Ken, *350 Miles: an Essex Journey*, Essex County Council, 2005

Dorset History Centre:

'Proposed House for H M Tomlinson Esq', 1931 DC-BTR/BC/1931/21

Sale catalogue for the Chesil Beach Estate, 1934 D-COO/J/214

Fox Strangways (Earls of Ilchester) Estate Archive (D/FSI) Box 152

Sale of old coastguard station, 1924 D/HAS/SP/1924/6

Bridport Local History Centre

Full Circle, the Othona Community Newsletter

Parish Church of St Mary, Puncknowle, church guide, undated

Deadman's Bay

Angel, John, *Diary*, see Wollage, Bob, *Soft burr and whitbed*, 1979

Barnes, William, *A Glossary of the Dorset Dialect*, Toucan Press, second edition, 1970

Bettey, J H, *The Island and Royal Manor of Portland*, 1750-1851, University of Bristol, 1970

Davey, George, *Memories*, privately published and undated.

Davies, Peter, *Art in Poole and Dorset*, Poole Historical Trust, 1987

Elliott, John Thomas, *Diaries*, see Wollage, Bob, *Slatts and Slubb*, 1976

Ellis, Clarence, *The Pebbles on the Beach*, Faber, 1954

Hardy, Florence, *The Life of Thomas Hardy*, Macmillan, 1928

Hardy, Thomas, *The Well-Beloved*, Osgood, McIlvaine, 1897

Ingrams, Richard & Piper, John, *Piper's Places*, Chatto & Windus, 1983

MacVay, Michael, obituary of Nancy Carline, *Guardian*, November 19th 2004

Morland, Joanna, *New Milestones*, Common Ground, 1988

Morris, Stuart, *Portland an Illustrated History*, Dovecote Press, 1985

Morris, Stuart, *Portland in Old Picture Postcards*, European Library, 1983

Nash, Paul, *Dorset Shell Guide*, Faber, [1936]

Nash, Paul, *Fertile Image*, Faber, 1975

Pentin, Herbert, 'Old Portland', *Proceedings* 37, 1916

Pitman, Jill, 'The Easton Massacre', undated

Powys, John Cowper, *Weymouth Sands*, Simon and Schuster, 1934

Ribbons, Phyllis, 'Ranters Lodge and the Dead House', *Dorset* May 2001

Ricketts, Eric, *The Buildings of Old Portland*, 1979

Saunders, Kathleen Winter, *A Child of Chiswell Remembers*, 1986

Toms, Cyril, *The Seiners and the Knocker Up*, 1994

Wollage, Bob, *Gallats and Scafflin'*, 1975

Wollage, Bob, *Slatts and Slubb*, 1976

Wollage, Bob, *Soft burr and whitbed*, 1979

Chiswell Visitor Information and Map, 2007

Friends of St Andrew's, *Avalanche and Forest*, 1977
Parish of All Saints with St Edmund, Wyke Regis, Church guide, 1999–2009
'*Some Interesting Headstones of St George Reforne*', undated

Conversation with Tom Neilson, 12/2/16
Conversation with Janey and Francis Carline, 29/2/16
Information about the whereabouts of John Cowper Powys's ashes provided by Charles Lock. (OS reference SY 560845)

Leaving the Island: Ferry Bridge

Attwooll, Maureen, *Bumper Book of Weymouth*, Halsgrove, 2006
Arkell, W J, 'Names of the Strata in the Purbeck and Portland Stone Quarries', *Proceedings* 66, 1948
Free Portland News 387, January 2011
Hardy, Thomas, *The Well-Beloved*, Osgood, McIlvaine, 1897
Lucking, J H, *Dorset Railways*, Dovecote Press, 1982
Morris, Stuart, *Portland an Illustrated History*, Dovecote Press, 1985
Portland Year Book and Island Record 1905, Centennial Edition, Friends of Portland Museum, 2004
Saunders, Kathleen Winter, *A Child of Chiswell Remembers*, 1986
Smith, Ron, 'Names to Remember', pamphlet, undated
Southern Times, April 24 1937
Sparks, Major W, 'Langton Herring', *Proceedings* 14, 1893
'The Wanderer', 'Portland's Fun Fair', *Dorset Evening Echo*, November 3rd 1961
Wollage, Bob, *Soft burr and whitbed*, 1979

Dorset History Centre:
Weymouth Port Sanitary Authority, Inspectors' Journal;
Sanitary Hospital plans D/CMY/482

Portland Heritage Trust Study Centre:
Account by Ken Saunders of Portland Fair, 1991
Files on the Weymouth Port Sanitary Hospital
Information supplied by Shirley Mitchell 14/4/16; 27/7/18

Information panels in Portland Museum, Wakeham

LAGOON

Anon, 'The Tides of the Fleet', *Proceedings* 26, 1905
Atkinson, E H Tindal, 'Some Abbotsbury Records'[oysters], *Proceedings* 48, 1927
Bailey, C J, 'An Early Iron Age 'B' Hearth Site Indicating Salt Working on the North Shore of the Fleet at Wyke Regis', *Proceedings* 8, 1962
Bird, Eric C F, 'A 17th century attempt to drain the Fleet', *Dorset* 17, 1971
Bird, Eric, C F, 'The Lost Wall', Dorset 21, 1971
Cornish, Vaughan, 'On the Grading of the Chesil Beach Shingle', *Proceedings 19*, 1898
Darton, F J Harvey, *Alibi Pilgrimage*, Newnes 1936
Good, Ronald, *Weyland*, Friary Press, 1945
Hollings, Doug, *All about Ferrybridge*, 1993
Hollings, Doug, *A History of Wyke Regis*, 2002
Ilchester, Earl of, Letter of Dec 23 1926, *Proceedings* 48, 1927
Le Pard, Gordon, 'The Draining of the Fleet', *Proceedings* 124, 2004

Littman, LTS, Ashley Chase. *A Dorset Domain*, Alan Sutton, 1988
Ordnance Survey geological map of West Fleet, sheet 341/342
Palmer, Susan, 'Neolithic Sites on the Floor of the Fleet', *Proceedings* 84, 1962
Richardson, Nelson M, 'The Travels of Peter Mundy in Dorset in 1635', *Proceedings* 42, 1922
Sparks, Major W, 'Langton Herring', *Proceedings* 14, 1893
Taylor, Christopher, *Dorset*, Hodder and Stoughton, 1970

'The Fleet Lagoon', *Dorset Countryside*, undated
www.crabhousecafe.co.uk

A Lamentation of Swans

Beaumont, Cyril W, *Michel Fokine and his Ballets*, C W Beaumont, 1945
Barnes, William, *A Glossary of the Dorset Dialect*, Toucan Press, second edition, 1970
Bridport News, October 6th 2016
Darton, F J Harvey, *The Marches of Wessex*, Newnes, 1922
Defoe, Daniel, *Tour through the Whole Island of Great Britain*, 1724–26
Dictionary of National Biography, Oxford University Press, 2004,'Selous, Edmund'
Fair, John & Moxom, Don, *Abbotsbury & the Swannery*, Dovecote Press, 1993
Fair, John, *The Mute Swan*, Gavin Press, 1985
Fonteyn, Margot, *Pavlova Impressions*, Weidenfeld & Nicolson, 1984
Fowles, John, 'The Chesil Bank', *Dorset*, 1984
Gosse, Edmund, *Father and Son*, Heinemann, 1907

Hardy, Thomas, *Tess of the d'Urbervilles*, Osgood, McIlvaine, 1891
J A C W, Obituary of Edward Victor Tanner, *Proceedings* 99, 1980
Mansell-Pleydell, J C, 'Decoys and Swan Marks', *Proceedings* 8, 1887
Prendergast, E D V, 'The History of the Abbotsbury Duck Decoy', *Proceedings* 106, 1985
Selous, Edmund, *Bird Watching*, J M Dent, 1901
Selous, Edmund, *Realities of Bird Life*, Constable, 1927
Tennyson, Alfred, *Poems and Plays*, Oxford University Press, 1965

Dorset History Centre:

Fox Strangways (Earls of Ilchester) Estate Archive (D/FSI) Boxes 151–2

Weymouth Reference Library

McBride, Edward, 'Dr Andrew C Fenoulhet MD', undated paper

Information on display boards in Abbotsbury Swannery
Information on Edmund Selous and kind permission to publish his great-grandfather's memories and Thomas Hardy's letter to Selous, September 27th 1927, from Brother Hugh SSF, Hilfield Friary

Wikipedia entries on Wyke Castle and 'Le Cygne'

Abbotsbury Alibi

Darton, F J Harvey, *Alibi Pilgrimage*, Newnes, 1936
Darton, F J Harvey, T*he Marches of Wessex*, Newnes, 1922

De La Tour, Lillian, *Elizabeth is Missing*, Michael Joseph, 1947
Fielding, Henry, *A Clear State of the Case of Elizabeth Canning*, 1753
Grigson, Geoffrey, *The Shell Country Alphabet*, Michael Joseph, 1966
Tey, Josephine, *The Franchise Affair*, Peter Davies, 1975
Treherne, John, *The Canning Enigma*, Cape, 1989

Village for Sale

The most informed source for this chapter was:

Gale, Elizabeth Buckler, *Two Days One Summer*, Time and Tide, 2007

Bridport News, August 8th 1958
Collins, Andrew, *Still Suitable for Miners, Billy Bragg*, Virgin Books, 2007
Spurling, Hilary, *The Girl from the Fiction Department*, Hamish Hamilton, 2002
Treves, Frederick, *Highways and Byways in Dorset*, Macmillan, 1906
Western Gazette, August 8th 1958
Wildeblood, Peter, *Against the Law*, Penguin, 1957
Wright, Patrick, *The Village that Died for England*, Cape, 1995

Dorset History Centre:
Burton Bradstock sale catalogue, D-DSP 270/2 and D-H DS/SP/1958/10

Information supplied by Sophie Houlton, National Trust, October 3rd 2016

https://www.nationaltrust.org.uk/features/follow-the-history-of-our-places-with-land-map
Channel Four Film: *A Very British Sex Scandal*, 2007

ABBOTSBURY GARLAND

Baker, Richard St Barbe, *My Life My Trees*, Findhorn, 1970
Best, Andrew (ed) *Water Springing from the Ground, Anthology of Writings of Rolf Gardiner*, Springhead, 1973
Bower, Kathy, 'An old May Day celebration', *Blackmore Vale Magazine*, May 21 1993
Collis, John Stewart, *Bound Upon a Course*, Sidgwick & Jackson, 1971
Cooper, T, *Abbotsbury Guide*, 2nd edition, 1895
Cresswell, Ruth Alston (ed) *Spirit of the Trees*, Society of Men of the Trees, 1947
Davies, Glanville J, 'Dorset in the Newfoundland Trade', Proceedings 101, 1980
Dewar, Stephen, 'St Catherine of Alexandria and her Cult at Abbotsbury', *Proceedings* 90, 1969
Draper, Jo, 'Flowers, Fish and Traditions', *Dorset Magazine*, May 2013
Dunning, Brian, 'Land of Swans and Smuggling', *Country Life*, January 30th 1975
Gale, Elizabeth Buckler, *Farming, Fishermen and Flax Spinners*, 1983
Gardiner, Rolf, 'Memories of Abbotsbury', *Dorset Year Book*, 1971
Mayo, C H, 'Garland Day', *Somerset & Dorset Notes & Queries*, vol iii, 1893
Morris, Stuart, *Portland an Illustrated History*, Dovecote Press, 1985

Moule, W S, *Abbotsbury,* new edition, 1946

Northover, Douglas & Lovelace, Martin, 'The Language of Old Burton', *Lore & Language,* February 8th 1989

Old-Time Songs from Newfoundland, Gerald S Doyle, 1955

Ouseley, Maurice, 'Burton Bradstock', *Dorset Year Book*, 1951-2

Page, William, *Victoria County History of Dorset*, vol 2, Constable, 1908

Poulsen, Jeany, 'The Wonders of My Garden', *Dorset Magazine*, August 2008

Sherren, Wilkinson, *The Wessex of Romance*, Chapman & Hall, 1902

Sparks, Major W, 'Langton Herring', *Proceedings* 14, 1893

Strangways, John, 'Account of his estate in verse', *Proceedings* 54, 1934

Toms, Cyril, *The Seiners and the Knocker Up*, 1994

Udal, John Symonds, *Dorsetshire Folklore,* 1922

Wright, Patrick, *The Village that Died for England*, Cape, 1995

Dorset History Centre

Plight of Gate Farm Abbotsbury D-ENS/F1/3041

Tree-planting Scheme at Abbotsbury D-WAL/C/2/7/4

Bridport Local History Centre

Northover, Douglas, *The Language of Old Burton, Burton Bradstock, Dorset*. With notes by Martin J Lovelace

Ouseley, Maurice, Typescript of an unpublished book on Burton Bradstock,

'An Appreciation of Abbotsbury', companion document to the village plan survey, 1973

Springhead Trust website

TROUBLED WATERS

Attwooll, Maureen, *The Bumper Book of Weymouth*, Halsgrove, 2006

Barnes, William, *A Few Words on the Advantages of a More Common Adoption of the Mathematics as a Branch of Education or Subject of Study*, Whittaker & Co, 1834

Bridport and Lyme Regis News, May 23rd 2013

Bryson, Bill, *The Road to Little Dribbling*, Doubleday, 2015

Chedzoy, Alan, *The People's Poet*, History Press, 2010

Dorset Life, April 2008

Grey, Edwyn, *The Devil's Device: Story of the Invention of the Torpedo*, Seeley Service & Co, 1975

Hearl, Trevor R, *William Barnes the Schoolmaster*, Friary Press 1966

Hollings, Doug, *A History of Wyke Regis*, 2002

Lloyd, Rachel, *Dorset Elizabethans*, John Murray, 1967

McDermott, James, *Martin Frobisher, Elizabethan Privateer*, Yale University Press, 2001

Pevsner, Nickolaus, *Dorset*, Penguin, 1972

Stinton, Judith, *Chaldon Herring*, Boydell, 1988

Dorset History Centre

DC-WYP/PHA2

Castletown D-Day Centre, Isle of Portland

Information on display boards in Abbotsbury Swannery

armada.parliament.uk

Burton Bradstock village website

Wikipedia entry on Major-General Shrapnel

www.bbc.co.uk 'The People's War – Langton Herring'

The Elm Tree

Baker, Hannah, 'The Spy Next Door', *Dorset Magazine*, January 2011

Betjeman, John, *A Few Late Chrysanthemums*, John Murray, 1954

Bulloch, John & Miller, Henry, *Spy Ring*, Secker & Warburg, 1961

Daily Mail, March 23rd 1961

Daily Telegraph, May 13th and 14th 1970

Fulford, Jack, *Dorset Echo*, May 12th 1970

Houghton, Harry, *Operation Portland*, Hart-Davis, 1972

Kennedy, Ludovic, 'The Portland Spy Case' in *Great Cases of Scotland Yard Volume One*, Reader's Digest, 1978

Letters from Springhead, Advent 1966

Lonsdale, Gordon, *Spy: Memoirs of Gordon Lonsdale*, Neville Spearman, 1965

Petridis, Alex, 'Next stop Culpho. Population: 40', *Guardian*, July 12th 2016

West, Rebecca, *The New Meaning of Treason*, Viking Press, 1964

National Archives.

Papers on Houghton and Gee, 2017: KV 2/4377;
KV 2/4380- 85

Weymouth Reference Library

Papers on the Portland Spy Ring

Information supplied by Debbie Hughes, landlady of the Elm Tree, April 8 2016

Hayman, Darren, *Thankful Villages* 1, CD, 12/07/2016
Vivian, Cecil, 'Lime-kiln Disaster'. cvivian@nfld.com
British Lion Films, *Ring of Spies*, 1964

WATER POWER

Beckles, Gordon, *The Bridport Story*, 1253–1953, Bridport Industries, 1953

Gale, Elizabeth Buckler, *Farming, Fishermen and Flax Spinners*, 1983

Gale, Elizabeth Buckler, *Two Days One Summer*, Time and Tide, 2007

Gardiner, Rolf, 'Slape Flax' in Best, Andrew (ed) *Water Springing from the Ground*, Anthology of Writings of Rolf Gardiner, Springhead, 1973

Kerr, Barbara, *Bound to the Soil*, John Baker, 1968

Pahl, Janice, 'Rope and Net Industries in Bridport', *Proceedings* 82, 1961

Phillpotts, Eden, *The Spinners*, Heinemann, 1918

Sanctuary, Anthony, *Rope, Twine and Net Making*, Shire, 1988

Sims, Richard, *The Rope, Net and Twine. The Bridport Textile Industry*, Dovecote Press, 2009

Sims, Richard, *Rope, Net and Twine. The Bridport Textile Industry 1*, Bridport Museum Trust, 2006

Stanier, Peter, *The Industrial Past*, Dovecote Press, 1998

Wright, Patrick, *The Village That Died for England*, Cape, 1995

Bridport Museum

Anthony Sanctuary Collection of Rope-making, and further information supplied by staff.

Bridport Local History Centre.
Northover, Georgie, *Historic Notes on Burton Bradstock*
Maurice Ouseley, unpublished manuscript on Burton Bradstock

Burton Bradstock village website

Conversations with John Willows, 2018

Pebbles

Ellis, Clarence, *Pebbles on the Beach,* Faber, 1954
Gale, Elizabeth Buckler, *Two Days One Summer,* Time and Tide, 2007
Palmer, Susan, 'Flint-Knapping Site at Abbotsbury', *Proceedings* 89, 1968

BBC film, 'Come with Me to Bridport', 1951

Index

PEOPLE

C

D

E

F

G

H

T

U

BUILDINGS

Abbotsbury shore (E V Tanner)